£4.99

Navigating Britain's Coastline

Land's End to Portland

Adrienne & Peter Oldale

David & Charles
Newton Abbot   London   North Pomfret (Vt)

Library of Congress Catalog Card Number 79-91496
© Adrienne and Peter Oldale 1980

Printed and bound in Great Britain by
A. Wheaton and Co. Ltd., Exeter, Devon.
for David & Charles (Publishers) Limited
Brunel House Newton Abbot Devon.

Published in the United States of America
by David & Charles Inc
North Pomfret Vermont 05053 USA

Great care has been taken in the preparation of this book, but the authors
and publishers regret that they cannot be held responsible for damage or
inconvenience caused by any error or omission that might remain. The
authors would be pleased to hear the views of users.

Acknowledgements

In producing this book we have received assistance and advice from many
sources. We would like to acknowledge this help with gratitude. In particular,
we thank the officers of the coastguard service who have assisted us in so
many ways with unfailing skill and courtesy.

We thank too the staff and masters of the harbours along the coast, in
particular Captain David G Banks and his assistants at Falmouth, where we
have been mainly based, and Captain G Hulland, harbourmaster of Penryn.

Finally, our thanks to the many seagoing friends who have encouraged us
in what turned out to be a more difficult undertaking than we expected!

Note: Coastguards

The coastguard services are constantly being improved, and certain of the
information given in this book may be changed. In particular, the duration of
watch at certain places may be altered. However, when any important
station is left unmanned, special radio links are installed to the nearest Marine
Rescue Sub-centre or Co-ordination Centre, so that calls made to the
unmanned station *will* be answered.

Introduction

This book arose from our own needs, discovered when we first began to sail extensively along unfamiliar coasts. It was then a constant problem to work out precisely where we were. On the chart we could see many objects marked 'conspic' — churches, hills, islands, headlands, etc — but it was not always easy to identify them on the shore. The churches seemed mostly to be buried in trees, there were often three or four similar hills, islands seemed to be part of the mainland, headlands looked like islands . . .

What we needed was some local seaman, familiar with the coastline, to point and say: 'That rock there — that's Kettles Bottom. And that headland sticking out is Bass Point. You can see the coastguard station on top.' At the same time he might put his finger on the correct place on our chart. This book aims to give just such help.

Three years ago we decided to make a guide to the coast by producing a book of 'views' that would show the whole coastline from a distance of a mile or two off. Under each view we would write useful information. Besides giving the shape and general aspect of the shore, we would also add enlargements of special items such as beacons, churches, lighthouses and so on. Finally, we would supply a simple outline 'chartlet' to aid in locating these items on your navigation chart.

We rapidly found that we had taken on a big job. To produce this first volume we have sailed in all some two thousand miles and taken hundreds of photographs. English Channel weather being what it is, there were days and weeks when no useful photography could be done. We would sail back and forth along a section of coastline peering out through the drizzling rain, creeping mist or blue heat-haze, vainly trying to pick out a particular hill we were assured was 'conspic' or 'easy to distinguish'. Coasts that faced westwards could not be photographed in the mornings. Coasts that faced eastwards could not be photographed in the afternoon. In choppy conditions considerable agility was required to hold a camera steady . . .

At last the photos were taken, and all of them were then combined to give a consistent series of views that could be carefully drawn to scale. Every drawing is backed up by a photograph taken from a carefully recorded place out at sea. Nothing is shown on the views unless we have actually seen it ourselves. Besides charted navigational objects, we also discovered items that were not charted, in particular the now ubiquitous caravan parks which are remarkably visible for long distances at sea, and these too we have included on our drawings.

Now that this first volume is finished, we hope you will find it a useful and welcome guide. It is impossible to imagine that, over such a long stretch of coastline, we have not made one or two mistakes, but we trust there are no major ones.

This book is not, of course, a substitute for careful navigation. The 'charts' are simply outlines of the coast, intended to help you find the particular stretch of coastline illustrated in the view. We do hope, though, that it will help you to identify the features of the coast as you pass along, not only making it easier to keep track of your position, but also adding further interest and enjoyment to voyages.

How to use this book

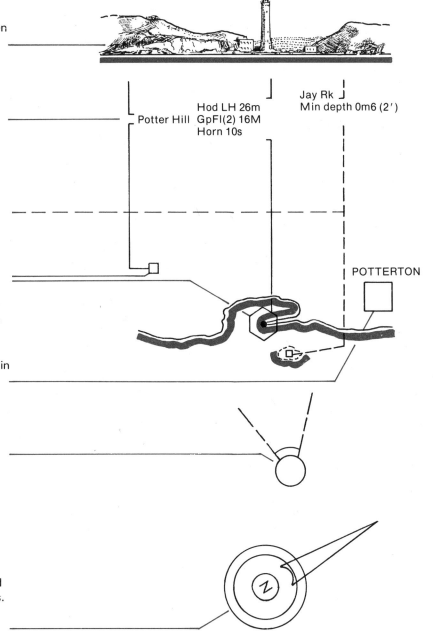

1   Every page contains at least one 'view' of a portion of the coast between Longships LH and the Portland peninsula. These have been prepared from specially taken photographs to give a complete picture of the main coastal features, landmarks, navigational marks, lights and harbours.

2   Below each view we give essential information about the places shown, with short vertical lines indicating their positions on the view. Where necessary to save space, the usual nautical abbreviations are used.

Potter Hill   Hod LH 26m   Jay Rk
GpFl(2) 16M   Min depth 0m6 (2')
Horn 10s

3   Where the wording refers to something not visible on the view the lines are dashed.

4   The descending lines lead to the objects' positions on an outline chart drawn below. Each line ends in a square except in the case of navigational lights which are marked by a hexagon.

5   THESE CHARTS ARE ONLY FOR IDENTIFICATION, TO HELP YOU FIND THE OBJECTS ON YOUR NAVIGATIONAL CHARTS. Scale approx 25mm = 1 nautical mile.

POTTERTON

6   Towns and villages are marked by larger squares: their names are given in CAPITALS.

7   Each chart has one or more 'eyes' drawn nearby. The circle marks the place from which the view was taken. The radial lines indicate its angular extent. A row of such eyes side by side indicates that the view above is a composite of a series of overlapping pictures.

8   Blue lines are drawn along the shoreline of each view, and round the corresponding sector of the coastline on the chart below.

9   On some pages two views are given, one above the other. Each has its own information written below. Lines from the top view are simply broken where they pass the bottom view. Where some object is visible in both views, a single line may connect the two with the chart below, but the written name will then be given under both views. The 'eye' for the upper view is marked TOP.

10   Further details, such as sectors of lights, harbour approaches, enlarged views of navigational marks, are inserted at convenient places on the pages.

11   NORTH is always UP unless a printed compass rose shows a different direction.

Comment utiliser cet livre

1   Chaque page contient au moins une 'vue' d'une partie de la côte anglaise depuis le phare de Longships jusqu'à la peninsule de Portland. Les vues ont été fondées sur des centaines de photos et montrent justement les traits de la côte, ses rochers, ses falaises, ses phares, ses ports etc.

2   Sous chaque vue nous donnons l'information essentielle sur les choses importantes qu'on peut y voir. Des lignes verticales montrent ces positions exactes. (Nous utilisons les abbréviations maritimes.)

3   En ce qui concerne les choses qui ne sont pas visibles sur la vue, les lignes sont interrompues.

4   Les lignes descendantes montrent les positions des objets sur une carte maritime simplifiée, imprimée sous la vue. Au bout de chaque ligne on trouve un carré; pour indiquer les phares, un hexagone.

5   DANGER! Utilisez les cartes SEULEMENT POUR IDENTIFIER LES OBJETS, afin de pouvoir les trouver sur vos cartes maritimes. Echelle approximative: 25mm = 1 mille marin.

6   Les villes et les villages sont identifiés avec des carrés plus grands. Leurs noms sont imprimés en CAPITALES.

7   Sur chaque carte on remarque des 'points de vue' dont le cercle est placé exactement où nous avons pris la photo sur laquelle cette vue fut fondée. Les lignes radiales indiquent les limites angulaires de la vue. (S'il y a plusieurs des 'points de vue', la vue est composée de plusieurs photos combinées.)

8   Les lignes bleues imprimées sous les vues et sur les cartes correspondent entre elles.

9   Sur certaines pages il y a deux vues, l'une au-dessus de l'autre. L'information pour chacune est imprimée au-dessous. Les lignes verticales de la vue supérieure sont interrompues par la vue inférieure. Si un objet est visible sur toutes les deux, le nom de l'objet est imprimé sous chacune entre elles. Les points de vue supérieurs sont representés par la marque 'TOP'.

10   L'information plus détaillée (par exemple, les détails à propos des phares importants et de la façon de s'approcher des ports) est imprimée sur les cartes dans les endroits appropriés.

11   Le NORD est vers le haut de la page, sauf quand on trouve sur la carte une rose de vents qui est orientée dans une direction différente.

Gebrauchsanweisung

1   Auf jeder Seite dieses Buches ist mindestens eine Teilansicht der Küste zwischen dem Leuchtturm von Longships und der Halbinsel Portland dargestellt. Diese Ansichten basieren auf Fotografien, die extra dafür angefertigt wurden, um ein vollständiges Bild der Gesamtküste mit ihren Landmarken, Seezeichen, Leuchtfeuern und Häfen zu geben.

2   Unter jeder Ansicht geben wir Erläuterungshinweise zu den jeweils dort vorhandenen Landmarken, Seezeichen usw. Ihre Position in der Ansicht wird mit kurzen vertikalen Linien dargestellt. Aus Platzgründen werden die üblichen nautischen Abkürzungen verwendet.

3   Wo sich die Erläuterungen auf solche Dinge beziehen, die in der Ansicht nicht sichtbar sind, ist die Linie gestrichelt.

4   Eine Verbindungslinie zeigt die entsprechende Position durch ein Viereck im Seekartenausschnitt an, der unter der jeweiligen Ansicht angedeutet ist. Bei Leuchtfeuern werden Sechsecke verwendet.

5   ACHTUNG: diese Kartenskizzen sind NUR dafür gedacht, das Auffinden der entsprechenden Orte in Ihrer Seekarte zu erleichtern. Ungefährer Massstab: 25mm = 1sm.

6   Die Namen der Städte und Dörfer sind mit GROSSEN BUCHSTABEN geschrieben.

7   Jeder Kartenausschnitt zeigt einen oder mehrere Standpunkte, von denen die jeweilige Ansicht gesehen wird. Der gekennzeichnete Sektor gibt den Blickwinkel an. Mehrere nebeneinanderliegende Standortsymbole bedeuten, dass die obige Ansicht eine Zusammensetzung mehrerer überlappender Bilder ist.

8   Blaue Markierungslinien auf der Seekarte bezeichnen den dargestellten Ausschnitt der Ansicht.

9   Auf manchen Seiten sind zwei übereinanderliegende Ansichten mit jeweils eigenen Erläuterungen dargestellt. Enthalten beide Ansichten dasselbe Objekt, wird dieses bei beiden Ansichten bezeichnet, und durch eine gemeinsame Linie mit der zugehörigen Position im Seekartenausschnitt verbunden. Wird die Bezeichnung des Objekts bei der unteren Ansicht *nicht* wiederholt, ist das Objekt nur in der *oberen* Ansicht sichtbar. Das zur obigen Ansicht gehörende Blickpunktsymbol ist mit 'TOP' bezeichnet.

10   Weitere Einzelheiten wie Leuchtfeuersektoren, Hafenannäherungen und vergrösserte Ansichten von Navigationsmarken sind an geeigneten Stellen der einzelnen Seiten eingefügt.

11   NORDEN is immer oben, wenn nicht anders angegeben.

Changes in coastal appearance from different viewpoints

The 'views' give accurate outlines of the coast, headlands, islands, prominent rocks etc as seen from the 'eye' positions. From closer in to the land, or from further out to sea, or from a distance to either side, their appearance will be different. The changes take place in predictable ways, enabling you to identify the coast easily.

FROM CLOSER IN TO SHORE the apparent height of the nearest parts of the coast will increase. The 'lighthouse' here is increased in prominence.
NOTE THOUGH THAT THE DISTANT BACKGROUND DOES NOT CHANGE MUCH.

THIS IS A DIAGRAM OF A TYPICAL VIEW SEEN FROM THE 'EYE'.

FROM FURTHER OUT TO SEA the foreground is reduced in apparent height but retains its general shape.
AGAIN NOTE THAT THE DISTANT BACKGROUND IS PRACTICALLY UNCHANGED.

When the coast is seen from further to left or right the foreground will appear to be shifted bodily the opposite way: the drawings below show the effect when the viewpoint is moved towards the middle of the page.

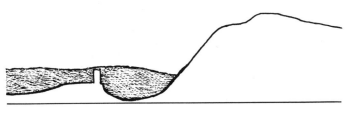

ACTUAL
VIEWPOINT

This is the effect if the actual viewpoint is to the RIGHT of the 'eye' on the chart.

This is the effect if the actual viewpoint is to the LEFT of the 'eye' on the chart.

The rule therefore is to divide the view mentally into FOREGROUND and BACKGROUND. Imagine the BACKGROUND UNCHANGED, with the FOREGROUND INCREASED IN SIZE (when nearer to shore), DECREASED IN SIZE (when further out to sea), or SHIFTED BODILY LEFT (when to the right of the 'eye') or RIGHT (when to the left of the 'eye').

Identifying coastal features

Lighthouses

A lighthouse at night is very conspicuous; by day, it may be a very different matter. Nor is the height of the light given on charts any sure guide to whether or not it will attract notice during the day. Berry Head Light is 58m high; Eddystone Light is 41m high. The Eddystone is a prominent, tall and graceful structure rising from the sea and visible for many miles. Berry Head Lighthouse, on the other hand, is quite a small building *on top of the headland.* It is the height of the headland which produces the very large height quoted on the chart. In all cases, therefore, we have given enlarged views of the light building.

Churches

Many of these are marked on charts as 'conspic'. We have found, though, that a number of them are difficult to discern, being lost among trees or buildings; our views, therefore, show only those churches which can still be seen clearly. The enlarged details show their outlines, in particular the shapes of their towers, as seen from two or three miles away.

Other Buildings

Rapid changes take place along the coastline and many buildings once conspicuous are no longer so. They may be hidden behind new developments or have near neighbours which are far more noticeable. We have only indicated buildings that can be seen and reasonably easily identified.

Harbour Works

It is surprising how unobtrusive can be the appearance of even large breakwaters, quays etc when seen from seaward, especially at high water. Usually it is the buildings of the town behind the harbour that can be seen most distinctly. In our approach views we have tried to indicate the position of the harbour entrance in relation to bigger objects in the neighbourhood.

Monuments

These are popular features with chart makers and indeed many are of great service to navigation. It is necessary, though, to know their shape and relative size. Often they appear much smaller than one might expect. A structure 20ft tall may be almost invisible, one 40ft tall little better, and even a substantial pillar 100ft high can seem quite trifling from a distance of two or three miles. Of course, to sailors familiar with the coastline, the small dark object on some distant hill may be immediately obvious and useful, but a newcomer could never identify it.

Islands

Charts show islands in plan shape and give little indication of their appearance. Our views all show the outline of islands or islets, which makes identification much easier. Nonetheless, they can frequently be totally invisible against a background of cliffs or other rocks. We have ourselves sailed 400yd off an island and been completely unable to separate it from its background.

Headlands

Just as islands may resemble headlands projecting from the coastline, so headlands may resemble islands from some angles. Each one has a characteristic shape. Berry Head, for example, has a very level top and a steep fall of 45° or so to seaward. Start Point has five rather jagged hillocks rising to the north of the lighthouse; Rame Head is conical, with a distinct ruined building on its apex. Since headland recognition is essential to good navigation, we have usually given several aspects of each one, as approached from different directions. Note particularly that the shape of a headland when it is very close is not a certain guide to its appearance from a distance.

Caravan Sites

These, with their large numbers of light-coloured vans massed together, are very easily discernible. They are frequently visible for several miles out to sea and may create a definite pattern which is identifiable from some distance. However, it is better to use the presence of a caravan park as confirmation of a position rather than as an identification mark in itself, since they are obviously subject to change in outline and size. All those we have shown are large and would certainly be visible in normal conditions.

Radio Masts and Towers

Though these are some of the largest objects on the coast, often several hundred feet tall, they are not so conspicuous as might be expected. The masts are extremely thin openwork structures, and at a distance of some miles are not easily picked out. In lowering visibility they are the first objects to disappear. Large dish-type aerials, however, are much more plainly visible, and those at Goonhilly can be seen and identified from many miles out at sea. Bearings on them are a positive and reliable navigational aid.

Military Installations

Certain military installations, especially radar scanners, are visible from seaward, but have had to be omitted from the views.

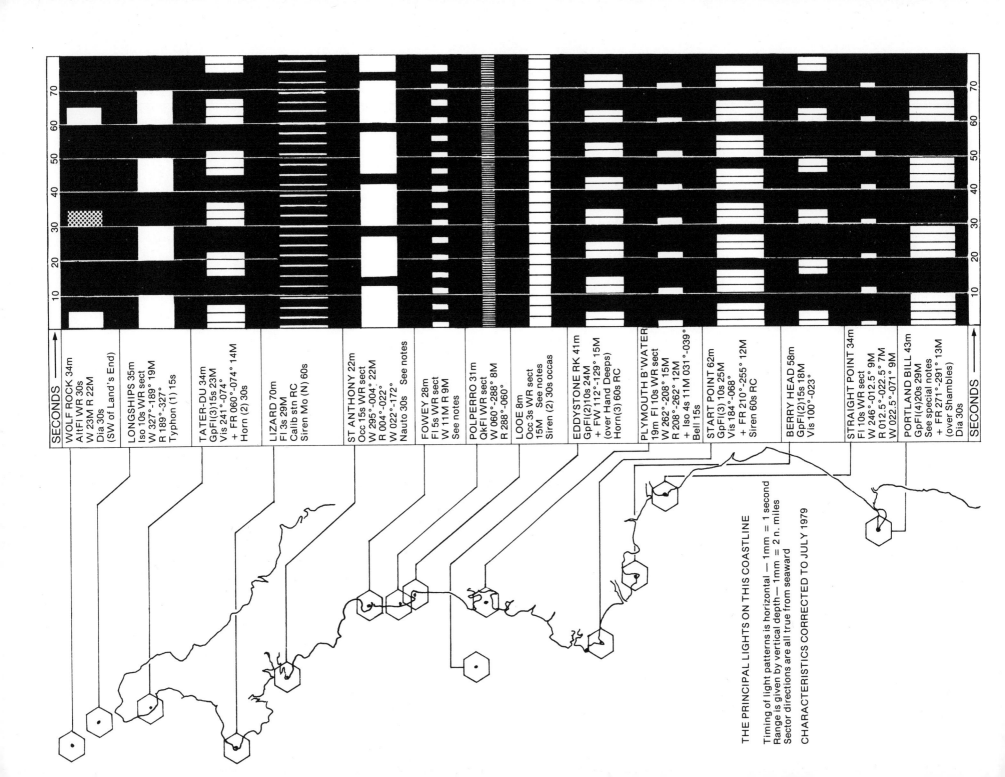

Glossary and Abbreviations

English	French	German	Dutch
approximate (approx)	approximatif	ungefähr	ongeveer
auxiliary (aux)	auxiliaire	Hilfs-	hulp
bearing	relèvement	Peilung	peiling
beacon (bn)	balise	Bake	baken
bell	cloche	Glocke	mistbel
black (Blk)	noir	schwarz	zwart
breakwater	brise-lames	Wellenbrecher	golfbreker
buoy (by)	bouée	Tonne	ton
can buoy	bouée cylindrique	Stumpftonne	stompe ton
castle (Cas)	château	Schloss	kasteel
channel	canal, chenal	Fahrwasser	vaarwater
church (ch)	église	Kirche	kerk
cliffs	falaises	Klippen	klip
coastguard (CG)	garde côtière	Küstenwache	kustwachtpost
conical buoy (stbd by)	bouée conique	Spitztonne	spitse ton
conspicuous (conspic)	visible, en évidence	auffällig	kenbar
diaphone (Dia)	diaphone	Pressluftsirene	diafoon
dock	dock	Dock	dok
dries	assèche	trockenfallend	droogvallend
east (E)	est	Ost	oost
entrance	entrée	Einfahrt	ingang
fixed beacon (bn)	balise fixe	feste Bake	kopbaken
fixed light (F)	feu fixe	Festfeuer	vast licht
flagstaff	mât	Flaggenmast	vlaggestok
flashing light (Fl)	feu à éclats	Blinkfeuer	schitterlicht
fort	fort	Fort	fort
green (G)	vert	grün	groen
group occulting light (GpOcc)	feu à occultations groupées	unterbrochenes Gruppenfeuer	groeponderbroken licht
harbour (Hr)	port, havre	Hafen	haven
head (Hd)	cap	Landspitze	voorgebergte
hill	colline	Hügel	heuvel
in line	aligné	in Linie	ineen
island(s) (Is)	île(s)	Insel(n)	eiland(en)
jetty	jetée	Anlegesteg	pier
quarry	carrière	Steinbruch	steengroeve
quick flashing light (QkFl)	feu scintillant	Funkelfeuer	flikkerlicht
leading light	feu d'alignement	Richtfeuer	geleidelicht
leading line	alignement	Leitlinie	geleidelijn
least depth	profondeur minimum	Mindesttiefe	minste diepte
light buoy	bouée lumineuse	Leuchttonne	lichtboei
lighthouse (LH)	phare	Leuchtturm	lichtvuurtoren
lookout	vigie	Wache	uitkijk
metre (m)	mètre	Meter	meter
monument	monument	Denkmal	monument
nautical mile (M)	mille marin	Seemeile	zeemijl
nautophone (Nauto)	nautophone	Membransender	nautofoon
north (N)	nord	Nord	noord
obscured	masqué	verdunkelt	duister
occasional (occas)	occasionnel	gelegentlich	nu en dan
occulting light (Occ)	feu à occultations	unterbrochenes Feuer	onderbroken licht
off-lying dangers extend...	dangers s'étendant... au large	Gefahren, die... vor der Küste liegen	voor de kust liggend gevaren reiken...in zee
orange (Or)	orange	orange	oranje
point (Pt)	pointe	Huk	punt
port	bâbord	Backbord	bakboord
radio mast	pylone	Funkmast	radiomast
red (R)	rouge	rot	rood
reef	récif	Riff	rif
rock (Rk)	roche	Fels	rotsgrond
seaward	vers le large	seewärts	buiten
second (time) (s)	second	Sekunde	sekonde
sector (sect)	secteur	Sektor	sector
shingle	galets	grober Kies	Keisteen
shoal	haut fond	Untiefe	ondiepte
siren	sirène	Sirene	mistsirene
south (S)	sud	Süd	zuid
starboard	tribord	Steuerbord	stuurboord
sunken rock	roche submergée	Unterwasserklippe	blinde klip
tower	tour, tourelle	Turm	toren
true	vrai	rechtweisend	rechtwijzende, ware
west (W)	ouest	West	west
white (W)	blanc	weiss	wit

Longships LH 45° ½M

Directions given are true from seaward

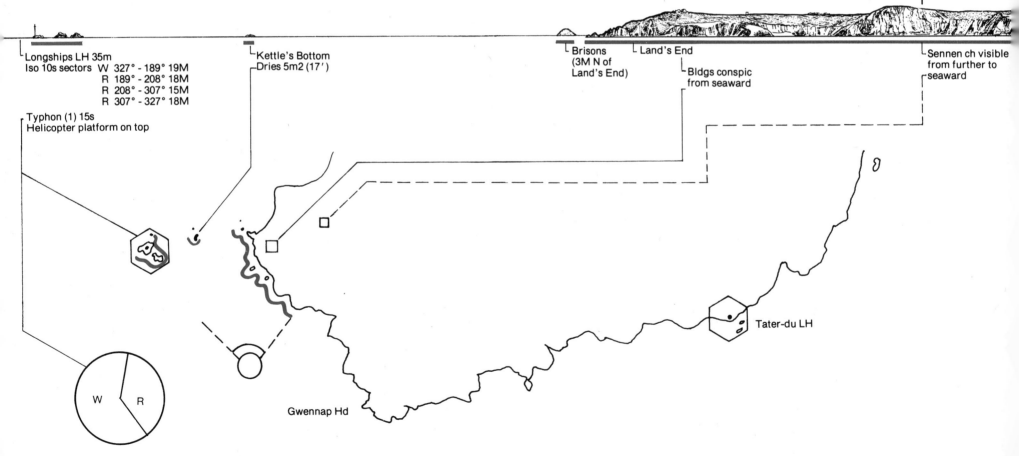

Longships LH 35m
Iso 10s sectors W 327° - 189° 19M
                 R 189° - 208° 18M
                 R 208° - 307° 15M
                 R 307° - 327° 18M

Typhon (1) 15s
Helicopter platform on top

Kettle's Bottom
Dries 5m2 (17′)

Brisons
(3M N of
Land's End)

Land's End

Bldgs conspic
from seaward

Sennen ch visible
from further to
seaward

Tater-du LH

W   R

Gwennap Hd

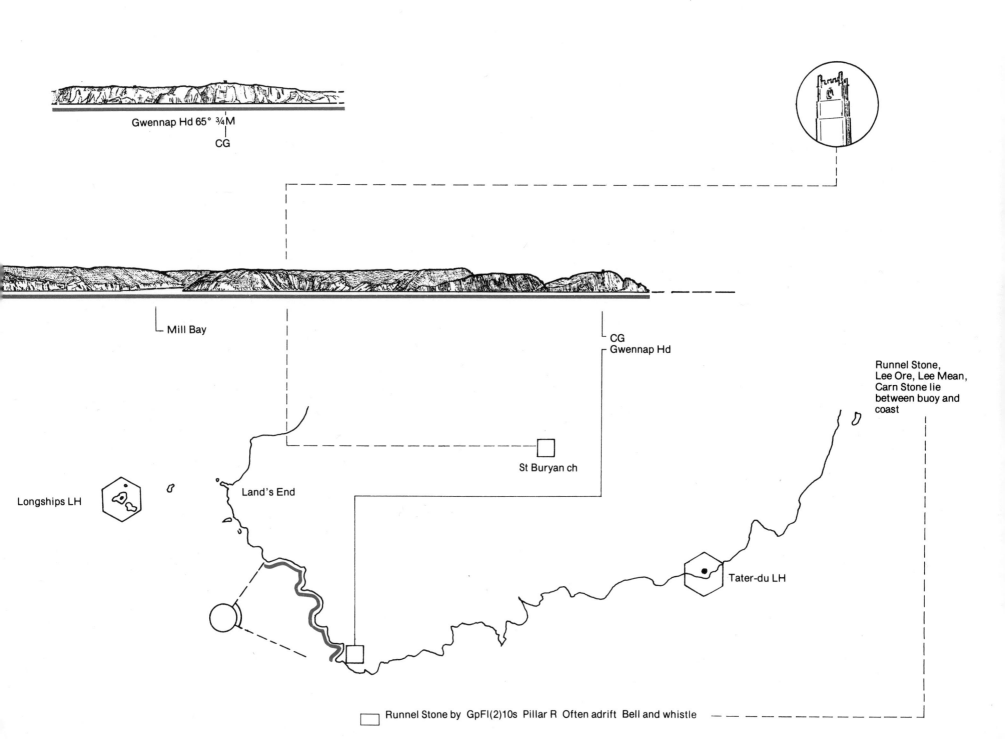

Gwennap Hd 65° ¾ M

CG

Mill Bay

CG
Gwennap Hd

Runnel Stone,
Lee Ore, Lee Mean,
Carn Stone lie
between buoy and
coast

St Buryan ch

Longships LH

Land's End

Tater-du LH

Runnel Stone by GpFl(2)10s Pillar R Often adrift Bell and whistle

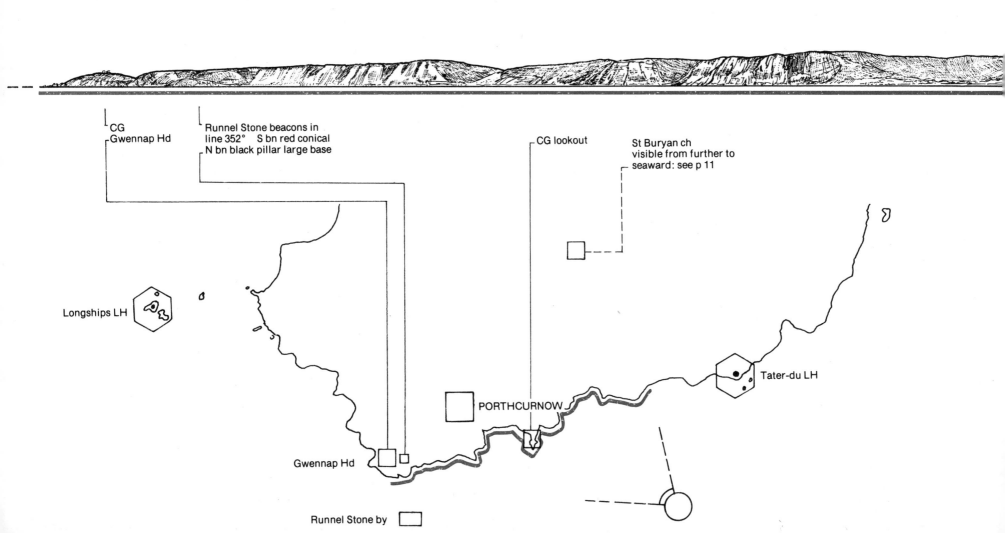

CG
Gwennap Hd

Runnel Stone beacons in
line 352°   S bn red conical
N bn black pillar large base

CG lookout

St Buryan ch
visible from further to
seaward: see p 11

Longships LH

Tater-du LH

PORTHCURNOW

Gwennap Hd

Runnel Stone by

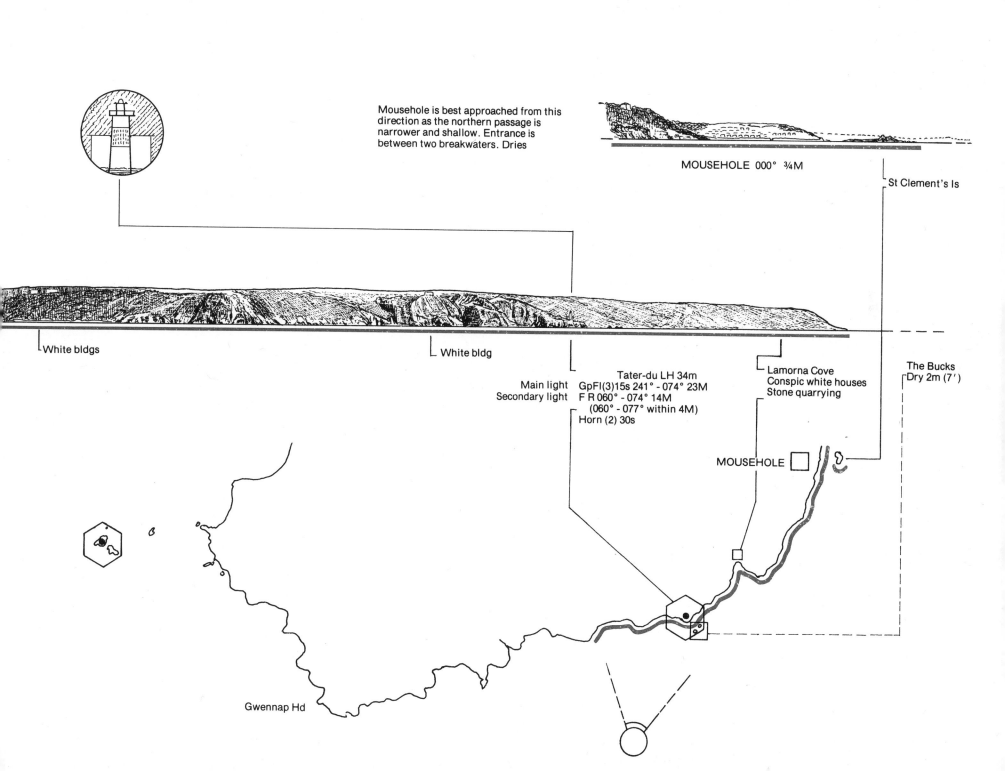

Mousehole is best approached from this
direction as the northern passage is
narrower and shallow. Entrance is
between two breakwaters. Dries

MOUSEHOLE 000° ¾M

St Clement's Is

White bldgs

White bldg

Tater-du LH 34m
Main light   GpFl(3)15s 241° - 074° 23M
Secondary light   F R 060° - 074° 14M
                    (060° - 077° within 4M)
                Horn (2) 30s

Lamorna Cove
Conspic white houses
Stone quarrying

The Bucks
Dry 2m (7')

MOUSEHOLE

Gwennap Hd

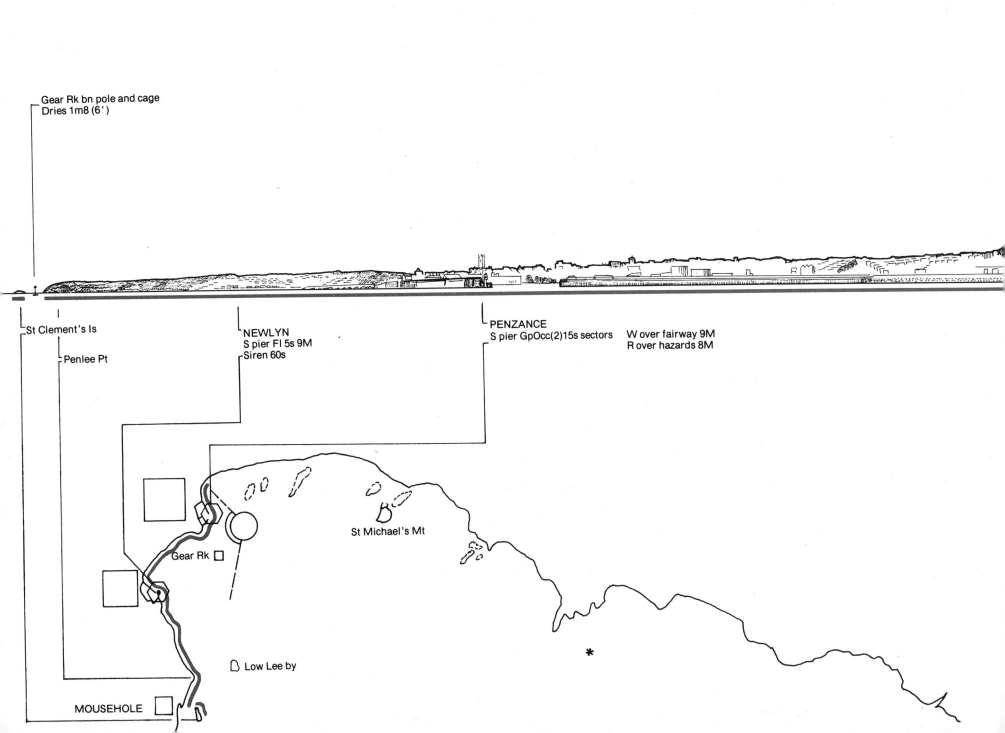

Gear Rk bn pole and cage
Dries 1m8 (6′)

St Clement's Is

Penlee Pt

NEWLYN
S pier Fl 5s 9M
Siren 60s

PENZANCE
S pier GpOcc(2)15s sectors   W over fairway 9M
                                R over hazards 8M

St Michael's Mt

Gear Rk

Low Lee by

MOUSEHOLE

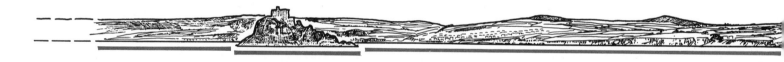

St Michael's Mt and Cas 350°
Harbour between Mt
and Marazion dries
Many rocks near approach

MARAZION

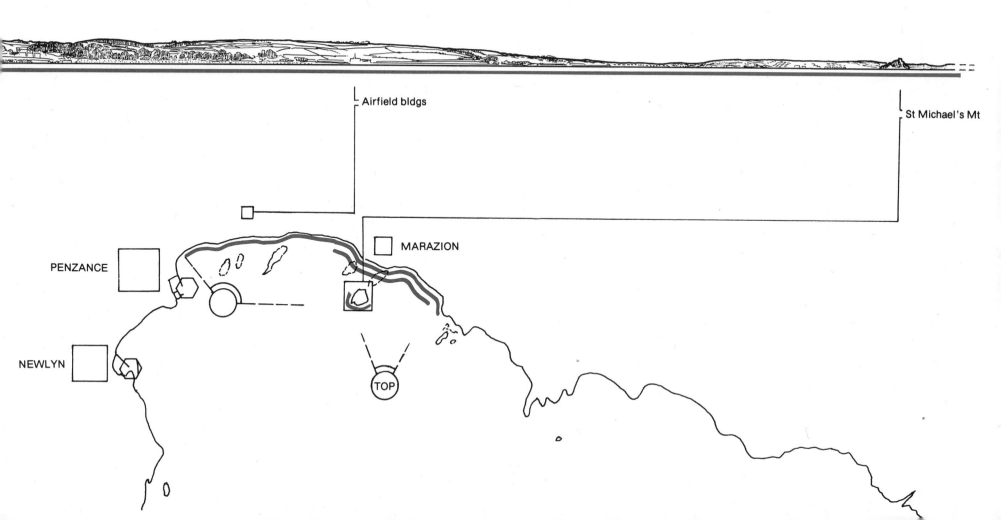

Airfield bldgs

St Michael's Mt

PENZANCE

MARAZION

NEWLYN

TOP

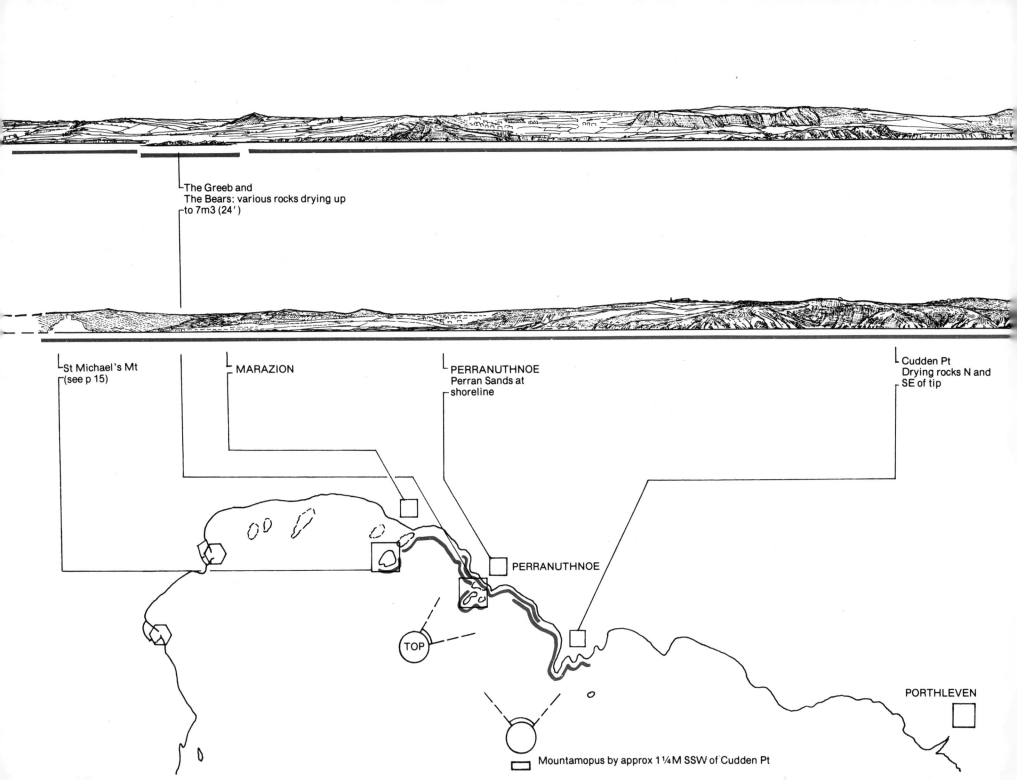

The Greeb and
The Bears: various rocks drying up
to 7m3 (24')

St Michael's Mt
(see p 15)

MARAZION

PERRANUTHNOE
Perran Sands at
shoreline

Cudden Pt
Drying rocks N and
SE of tip

PERRANUTHNOE

TOP

PORTHLEVEN

Mountamopus by approx 1¼ M SSW of Cudden Pt

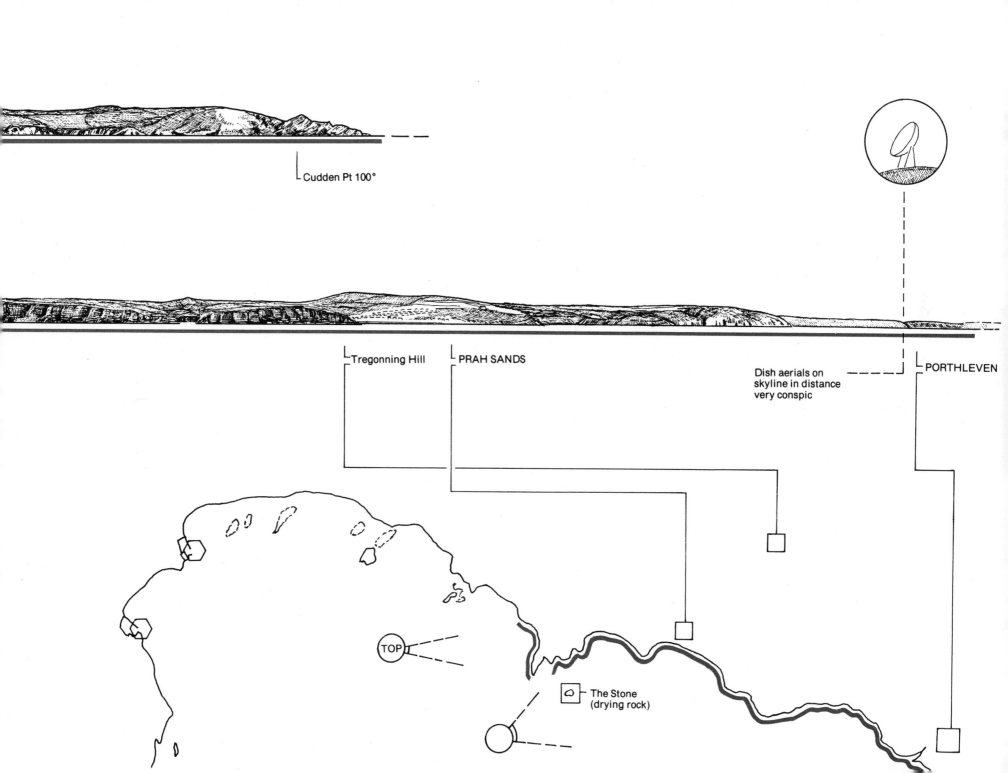

Cudden Pt 100°

Tregonning Hill

PRAH SANDS

Dish aerials on
skyline in distance
very conspic

PORTHLEVEN

TOP

The Stone
(drying rock)

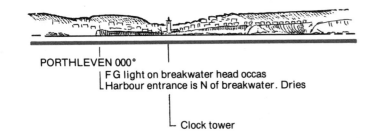

PORTHLEVEN 000°

| FG light on breakwater head occas
| Harbour entrance is N of breakwater. Dries

└ Clock tower

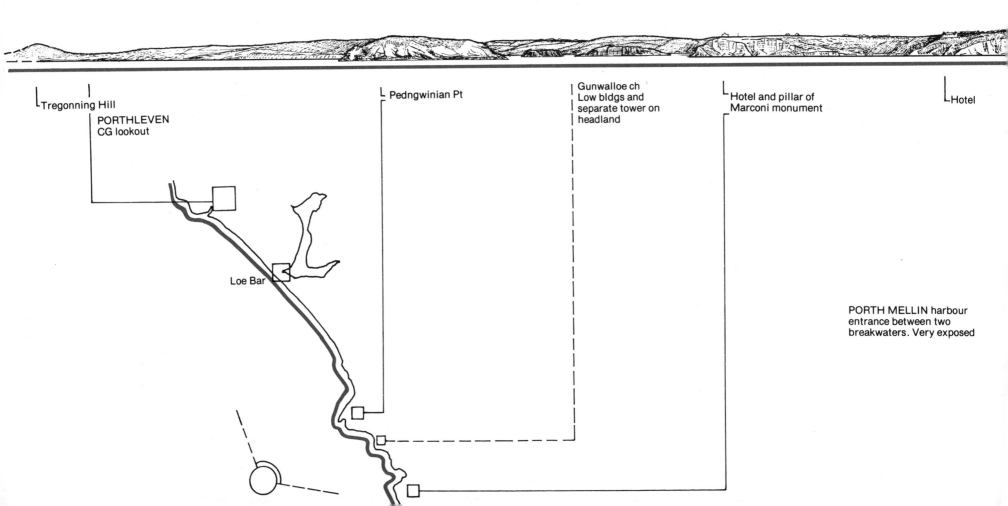

└Tregonning Hill

PORTHLEVEN
CG lookout

L Pedngwinian Pt

| Gunwalloe ch
| Low bldgs and
| separate tower on
| headland

| Hotel and pillar of
| Marconi monument

└Hotel

Loe Bar

PORTH MELLIN harbour
entrance between two
breakwaters. Very exposed

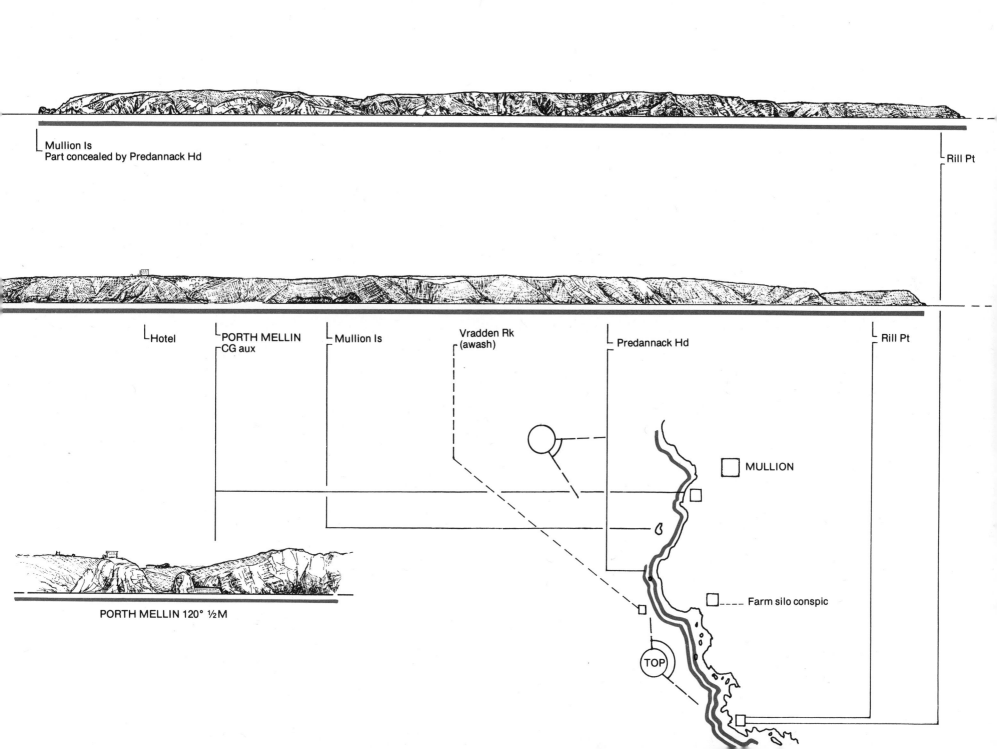

Mullion Is
Part concealed by Predannack Hd

Rill Pt

Hotel

PORTH MELLIN
CG aux

Mullion Is

Vradden Rk
(awash)

Predannack Hd

Rill Pt

MULLION

Farm silo conspic

TOP

PORTH MELLIN 120° ½M

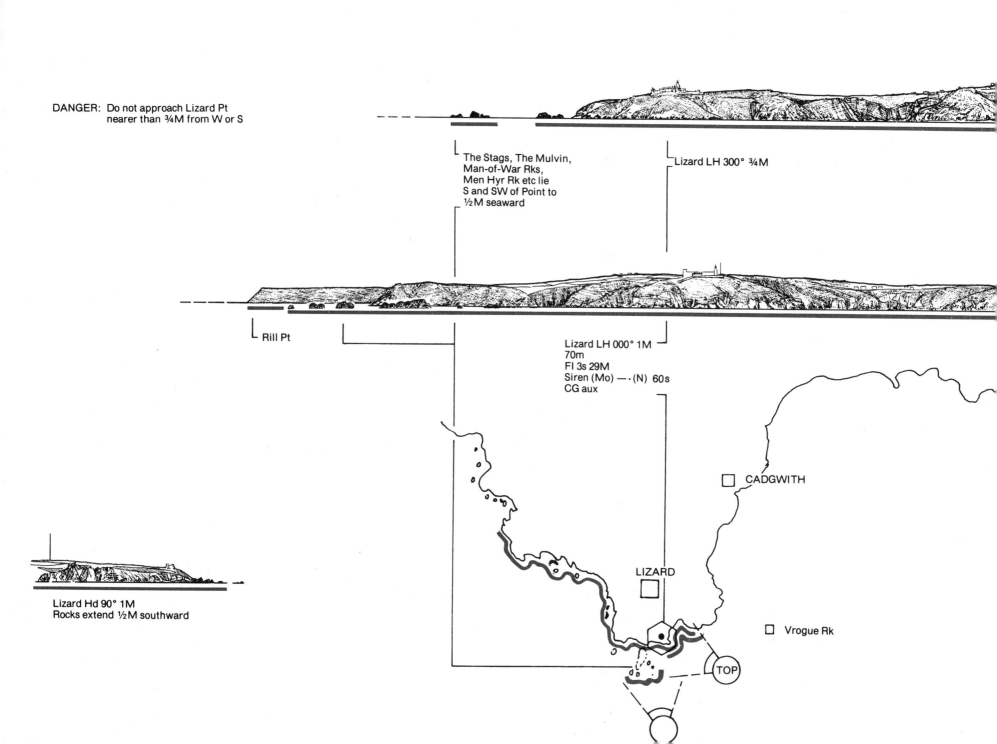

DANGER: Do not approach Lizard Pt
nearer than ¾M from W or S

The Stags, The Mulvin,
Man-of-War Rks,
Men Hyr Rk etc lie
S and SW of Point to
½M seaward

Lizard LH 300° ¾M

Rill Pt

Lizard LH 000° 1M
70m
Fl 3s 29M
Siren (Mo) —·(N) 60s
CG aux

CADGWITH

LIZARD

Vrogue Rk

TOP

Lizard Hd 90° 1M
Rocks extend ½M southward

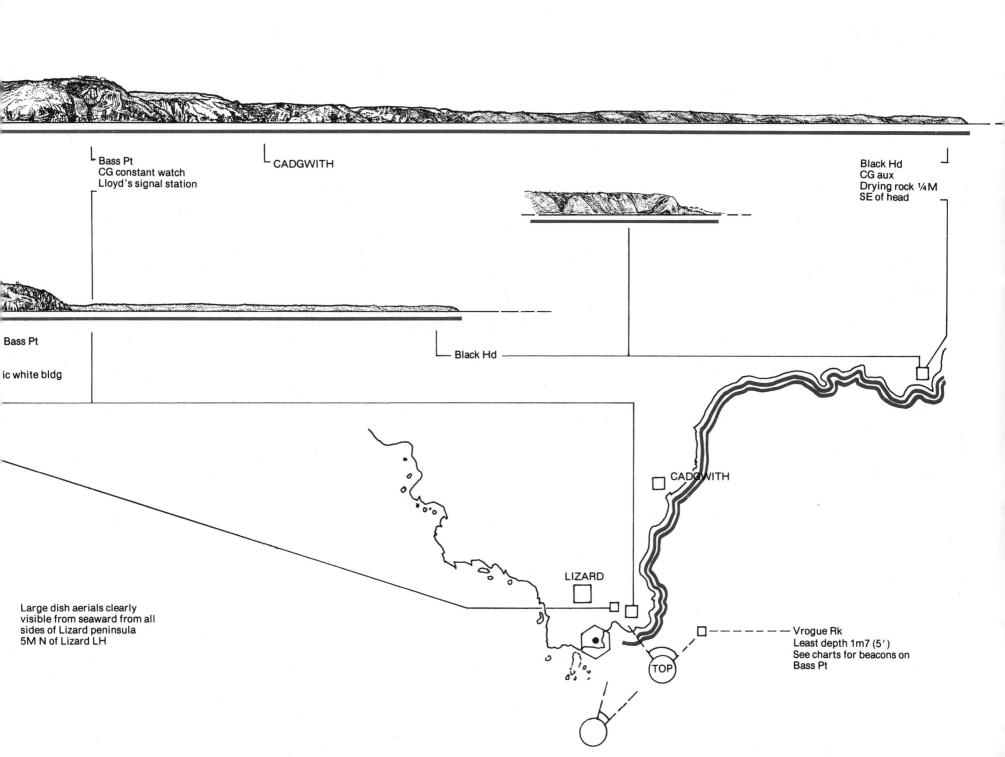

Bass Pt
CG constant watch
Lloyd's signal station

CADGWITH

Black Hd
CG aux
Drying rock ¼ M
SE of head

Black Hd

Bass Pt

ic white bldg

CADGWITH

LIZARD

Large dish aerials clearly
visible from seaward from all
sides of Lizard peninsula
5M N of Lizard LH

TOP

Vrogue Rk
Least depth 1m7 (5′)
See charts for beacons on
Bass Pt

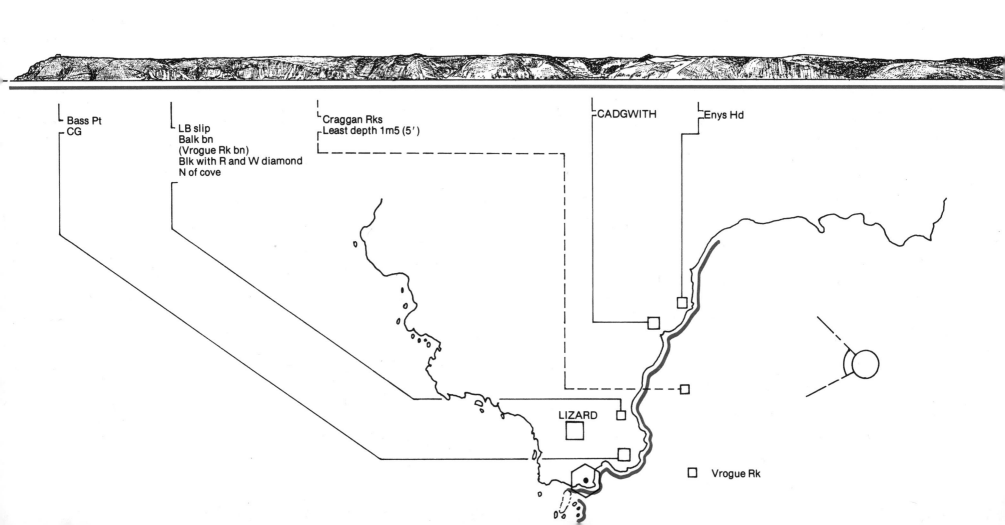

Bass Pt
CG

LB slip
Balk bn
(Vrogue Rk bn)
Blk with R and W diamond
N of cove

Craggan Rks
Least depth 1m5 (5')

CADGWITH

Enys Hd

LIZARD

☐ Vrogue Rk

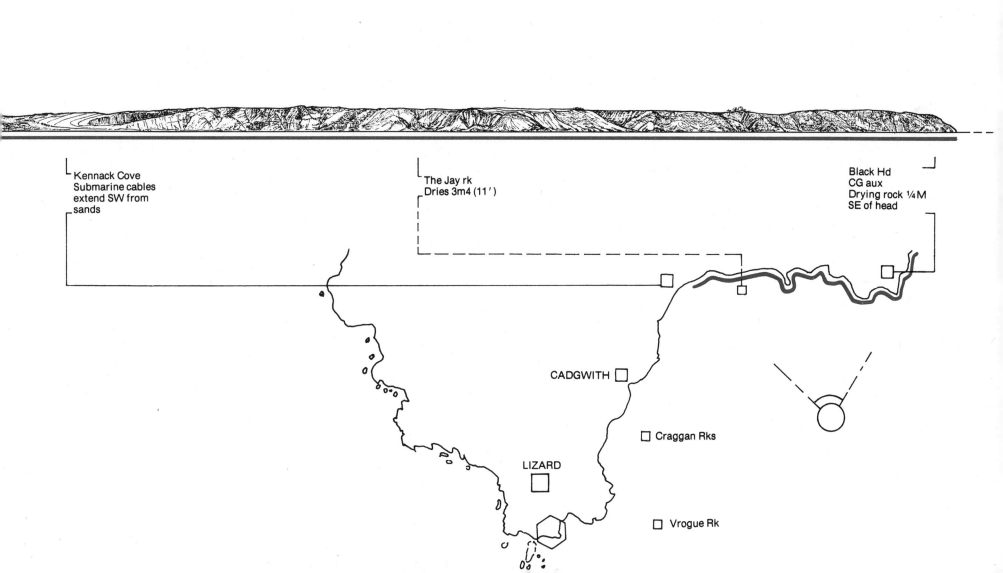

Kennack Cove
Submarine cables
extend SW from
sands

The Jay rk
Dries 3m4 (11′)

Black Hd
CG aux
Drying rock ¼M
SE of head

CADGWITH ☐

Craggan Rks

LIZARD

Vrogue Rk

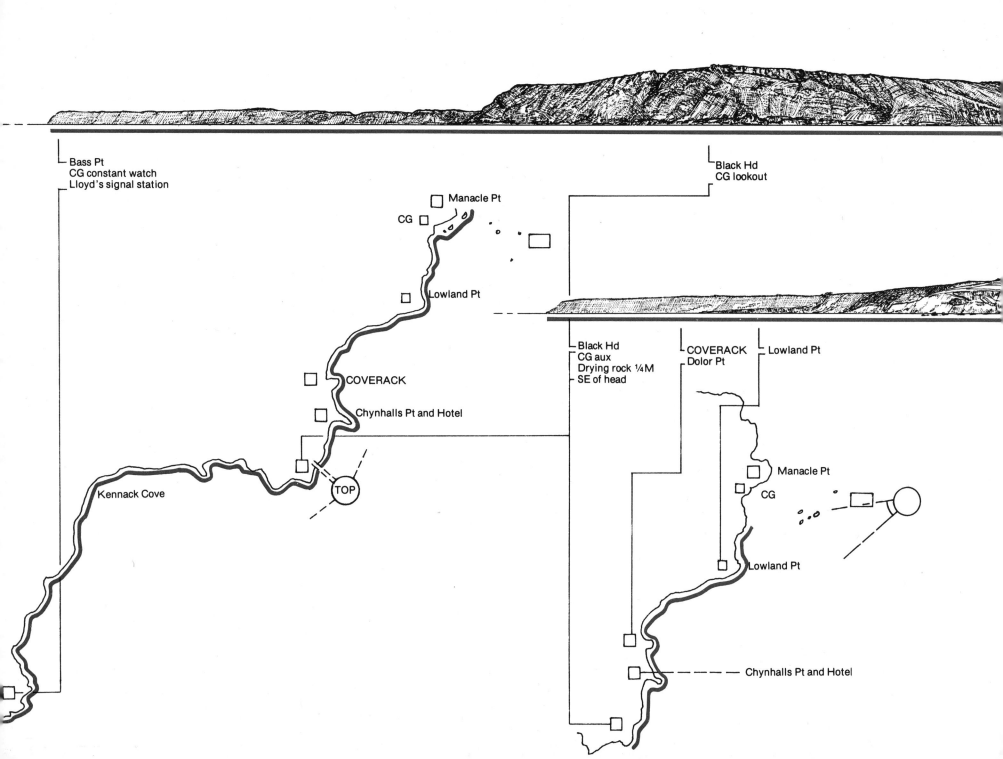

Bass Pt
CG constant watch
Lloyd's signal station

Black Hd
CG lookout

Manacle Pt

CG

Lowland Pt

Black Hd
CG aux
Drying rock ¼M
SE of head

COVERACK
Dolor Pt

Lowland Pt

COVERACK

Chynhalls Pt and Hotel

Kennack Cove

TOP

Manacle Pt

CG

Lowland Pt

Chynhalls Pt and Hotel

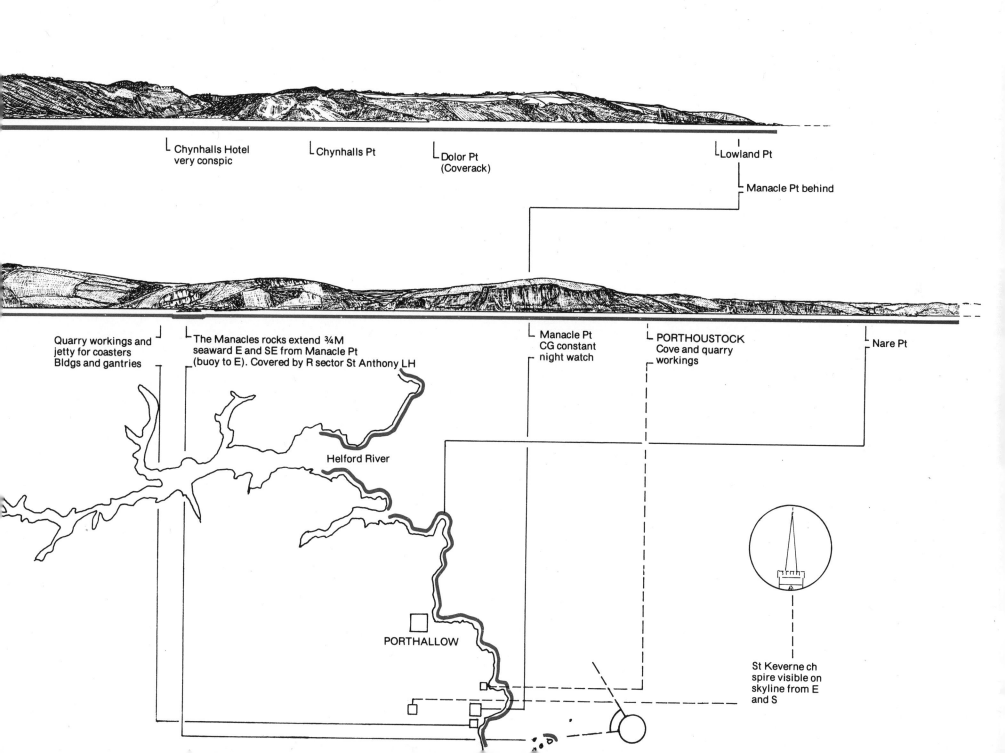

Chynhalls Hotel
very conspic

Chynhalls Pt

Dolor Pt
(Coverack)

Lowland Pt

Manacle Pt behind

Quarry workings and
jetty for coasters
Bldgs and gantries

The Manacles rocks extend ¾M
seaward E and SE from Manacle Pt
(buoy to E). Covered by R sector St Anthony LH

Manacle Pt
CG constant
night watch

PORTHOUSTOCK
Cove and quarry
workings

Nare Pt

Helford River

PORTHALLOW

St Keverne ch
spire visible on
skyline from E
and S

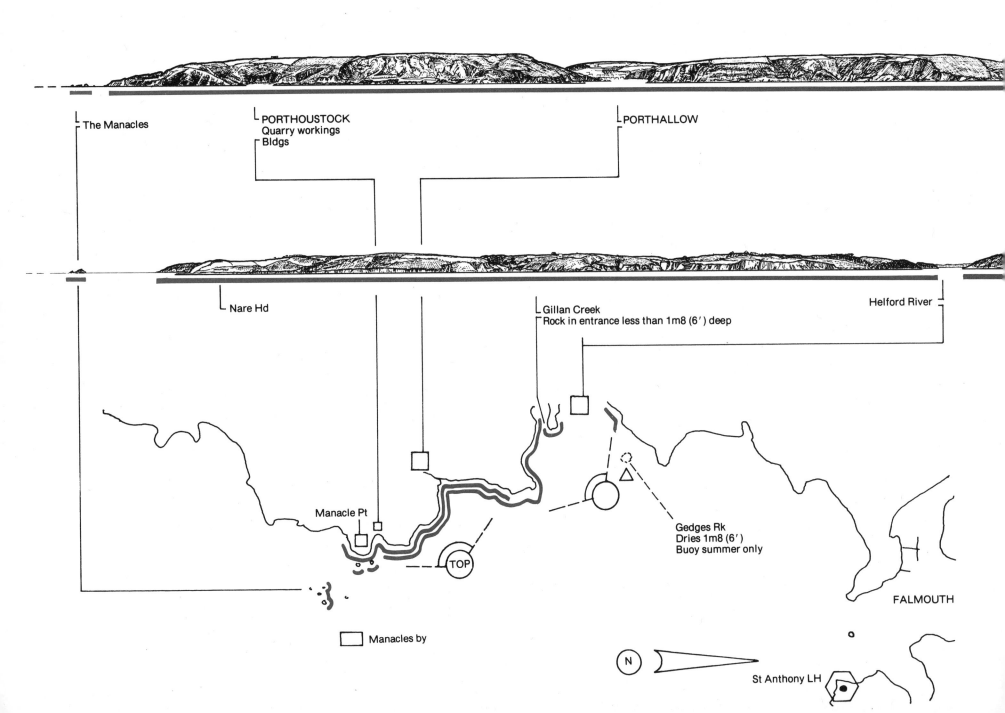

The Manacles

PORTHOUSTOCK
Quarry workings
Bldgs

PORTHALLOW

Nare Hd

Gillan Creek
Rock in entrance less than 1m8 (6′) deep

Helford River

Manacle Pt

TOP

Gedges Rk
Dries 1m8 (6′)
Buoy summer only

FALMOUTH

☐ Manacles by

N

St Anthony LH

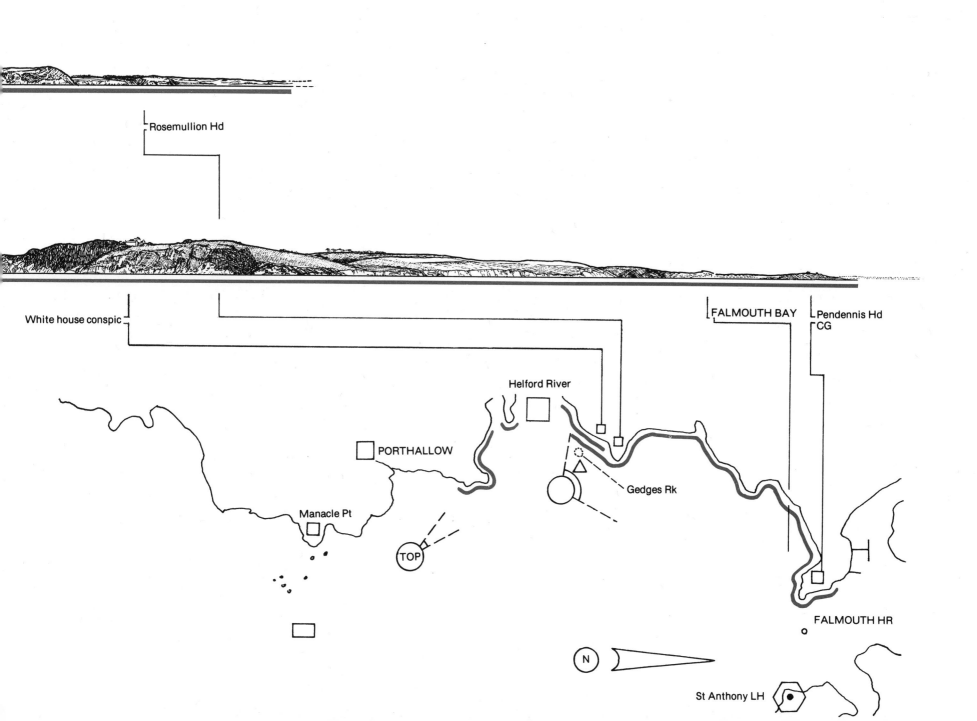

Rosemullion Hd

White house conspic

FALMOUTH BAY

Pendennis Hd
CG

Helford River

PORTHALLOW

Gedges Rk

Manacle Pt

TOP

FALMOUTH HR

N

St Anthony LH

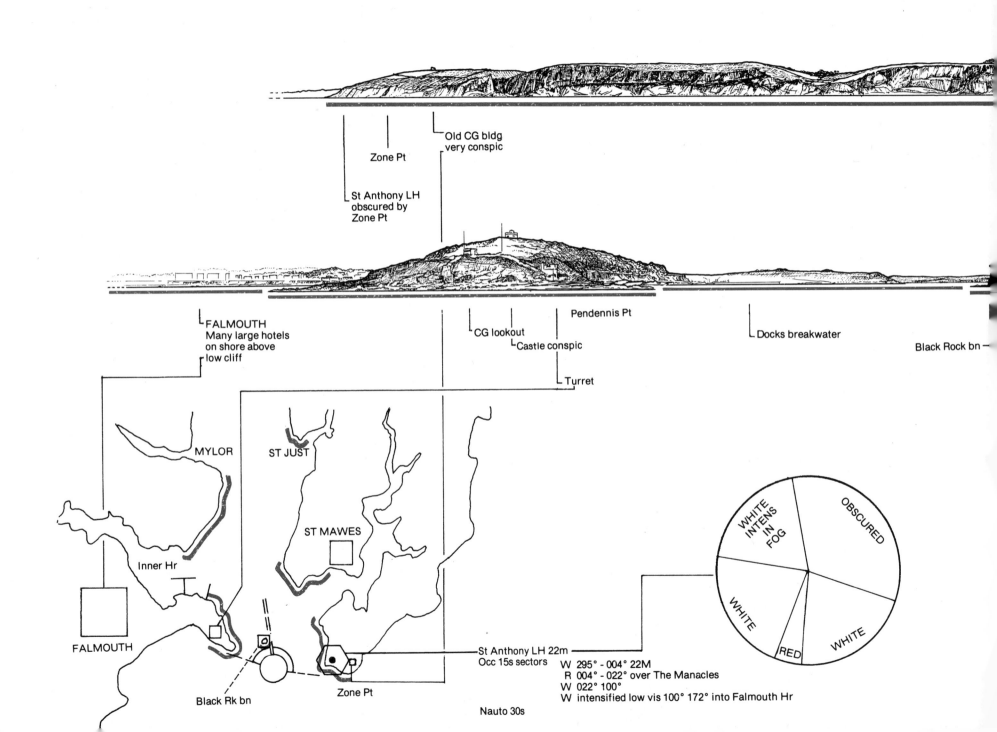

Zone Pt

Old CG bldg
very conspic

St Anthony LH
obscured by
Zone Pt

Pendennis Pt

FALMOUTH
Many large hotels
on shore above
low cliff

CG lookout

Castle conspic

Docks breakwater

Black Rock bn

Turret

MYLOR

ST JUST

ST MAWES

Inner Hr

FALMOUTH

WHITE INTENS IN FOG

OBSCURED

WHITE

RED

WHITE

Black Rk bn

Zone Pt

St Anthony LH 22m
Occ 15s sectors
W 295° - 004° 22M
R 004° - 022° over The Manacles
W 022° 100°
W intensified low vis 100° 172° into Falmouth Hr

Nauto 30s

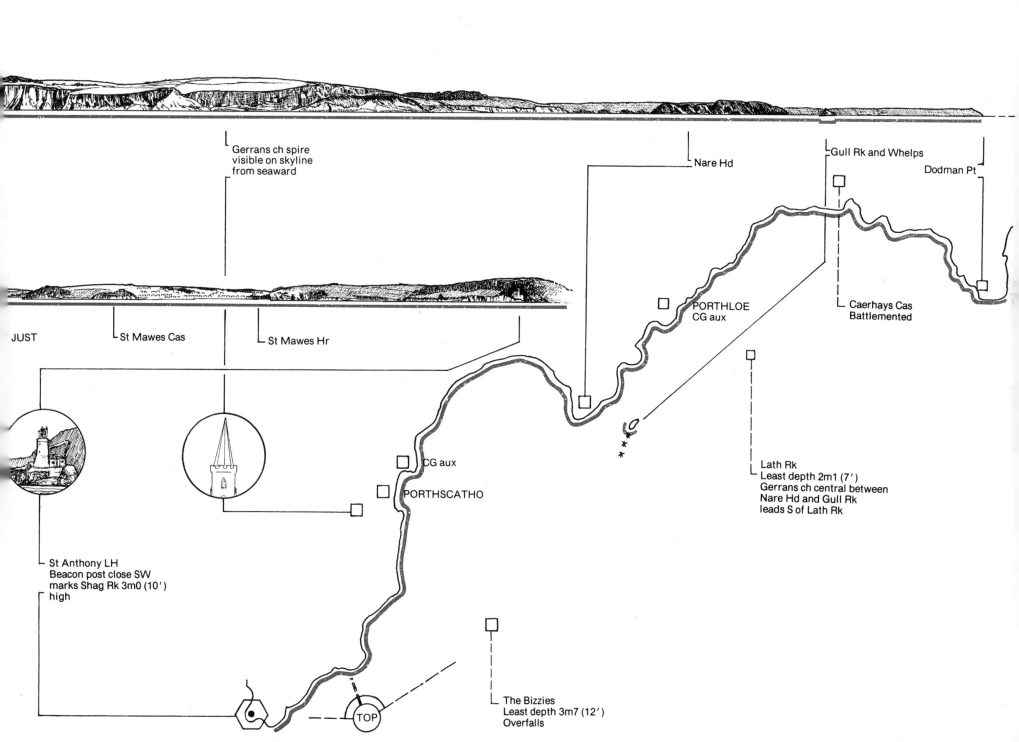

Gerrans ch spire
visible on skyline
from seaward

Nare Hd

Gull Rk and Whelps

Dodman Pt

PORTHLOE
CG aux

Caerhays Cas
Battlemented

JUST

St Mawes Cas

St Mawes Hr

Lath Rk
Least depth 2m1 (7')
Gerrans ch central between
Nare Hd and Gull Rk
leads S of Lath Rk

CG aux

PORTHSCATHO

St Anthony LH
Beacon post close SW
marks Shag Rk 3m0 (10')
high

The Bizzies
Least depth 3m7 (12')
Overfalls

TOP

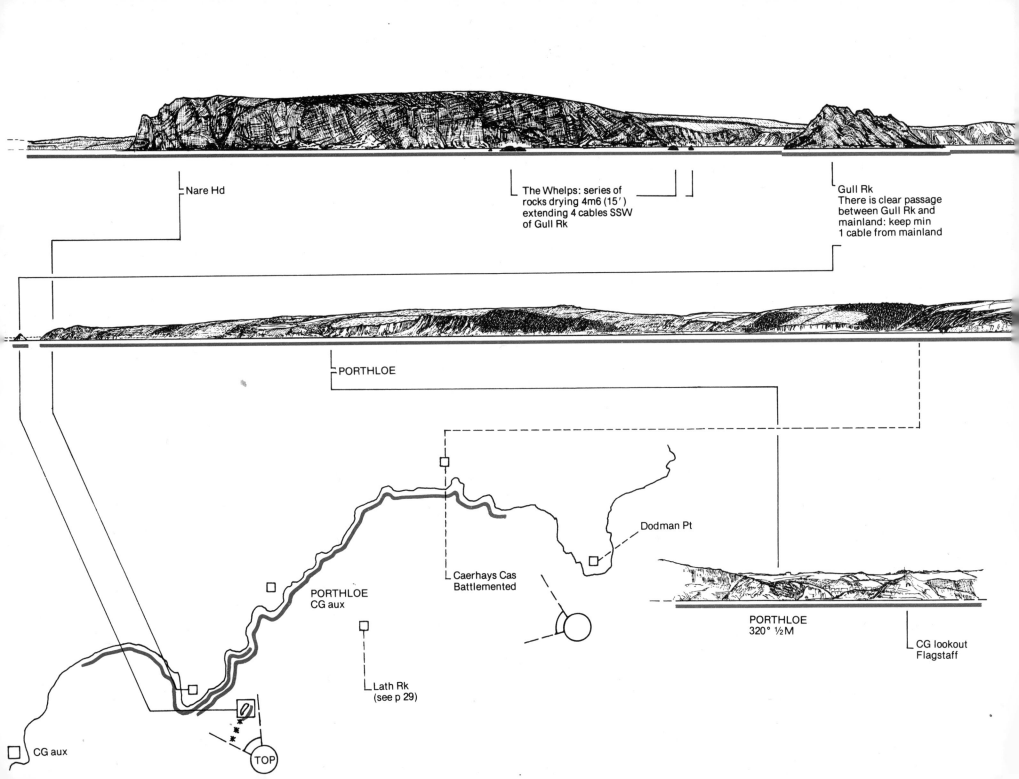

Nare Hd

The Whelps: series of
rocks drying 4m6 (15′)
extending 4 cables SSW
of Gull Rk

Gull Rk
There is clear passage
between Gull Rk and
mainland: keep min
1 cable from mainland

PORTHLOE

Caerhays Cas
Battlemented

Dodman Pt

PORTHLOE
CG aux

Lath Rk
(see p 29)

PORTHLOE
320° ½M

CG lookout
Flagstaff

CG aux

TOP

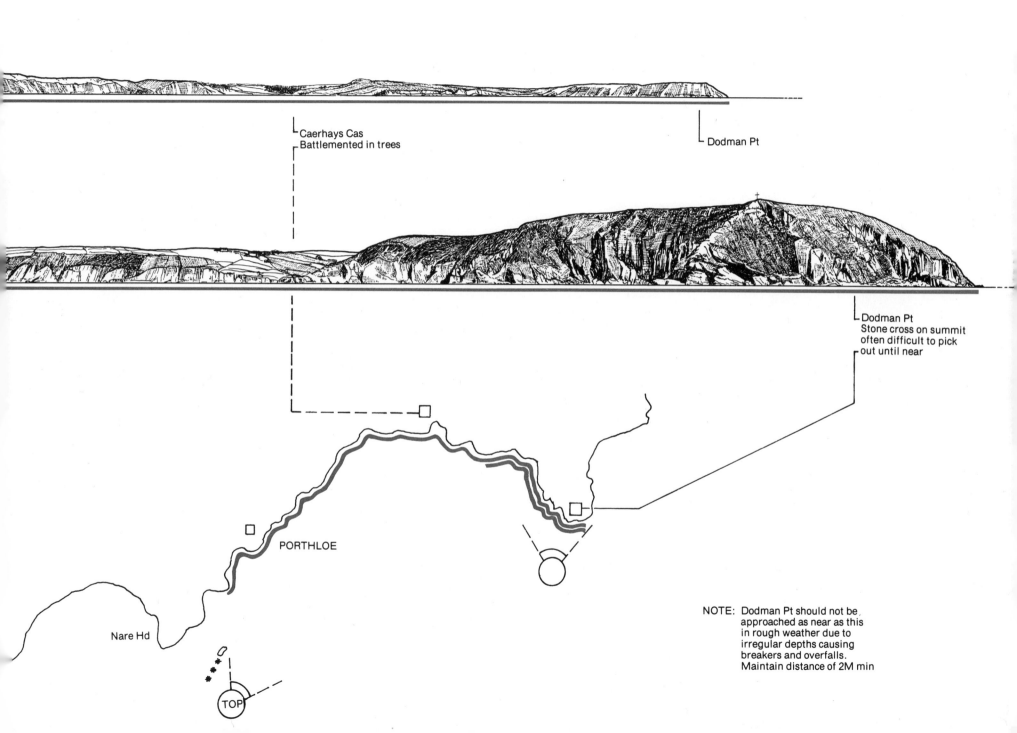

Caerhays Cas
Battlemented in trees

Dodman Pt

Dodman Pt
Stone cross on summit
often difficult to pick
out until near

PORTHLOE

Nare Hd

TOP

NOTE: Dodman Pt should not be
approached as near as this
in rough weather due to
irregular depths causing
breakers and overfalls.
Maintain distance of 2M min

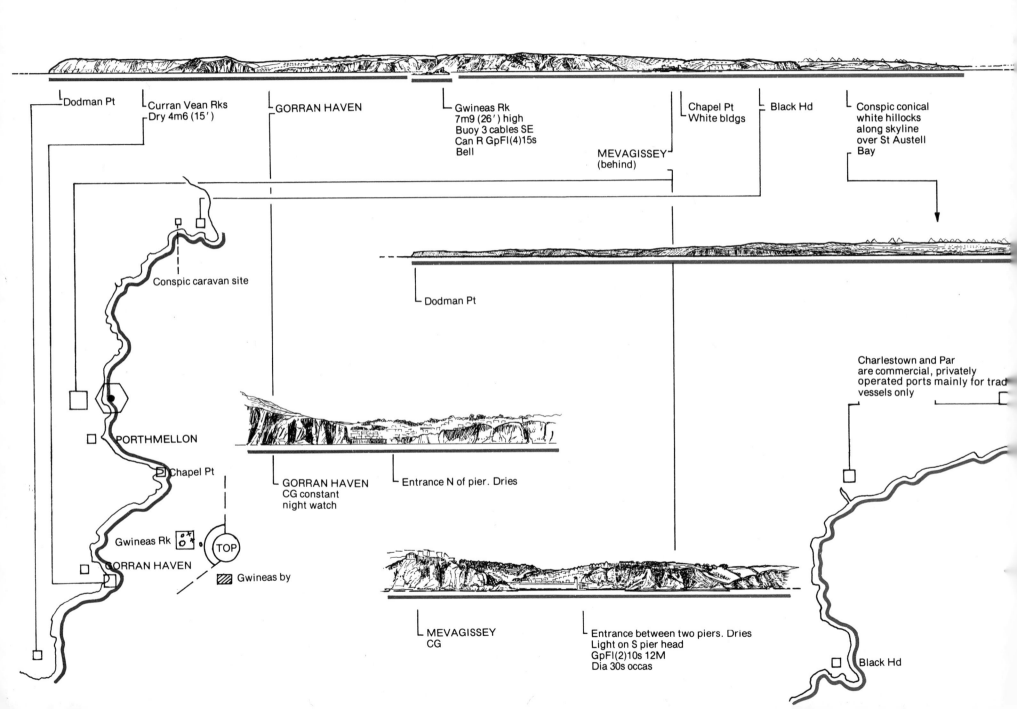

Dodman Pt

Curran Vean Rks
Dry 4m6 (15')

GORRAN HAVEN

Gwineas Rk
7m9 (26') high
Buoy 3 cables SE
Can R GpFl(4)15s
Bell

Chapel Pt
White bldgs

Black Hd

Conspic conical
white hillocks
along skyline
over St Austell
Bay

MEVAGISSEY
(behind)

Conspic caravan site

Dodman Pt

PORTHMELLON

Chapel Pt

Gwineas Rk

TOP

GORRAN HAVEN

Gwineas by

GORRAN HAVEN
CG constant
night watch

Entrance N of pier. Dries

Charlestown and Par
are commercial, privately
operated ports mainly for trad
vessels only

MEVAGISSEY
CG

Entrance between two piers. Dries
Light on S pier head
GpFl(2)10s 12M
Dia 30s occas

Black Hd

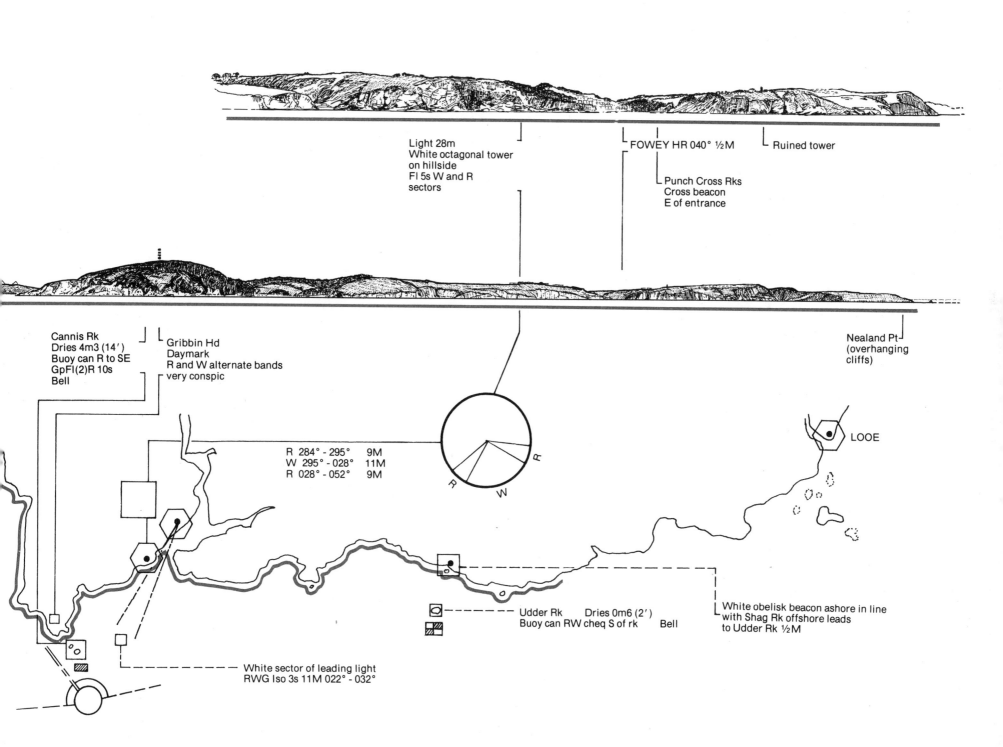

Light 28m
White octagonal tower
on hillside
Fl 5s W and R
sectors

FOWEY HR 040° ½M · Ruined tower

Punch Cross Rks
Cross beacon
E of entrance

Cannis Rk
Dries 4m3 (14')
Buoy can R to SE
GpFl(2)R 10s
Bell

Gribbin Hd
Daymark
R and W alternate bands
very conspic

Nealand Pt
(overhanging
cliffs)

R 284° - 295°   9M
W 295° - 028°   11M
R 028° - 052°   9M

R

R

W

LOOE

Udder Rk   Dries 0m6 (2')
Buoy can RW cheq S of rk   Bell

White obelisk beacon ashore in line
with Shag Rk offshore leads
to Udder Rk ½M

White sector of leading light
RWG Iso 3s 11M 022° - 032°

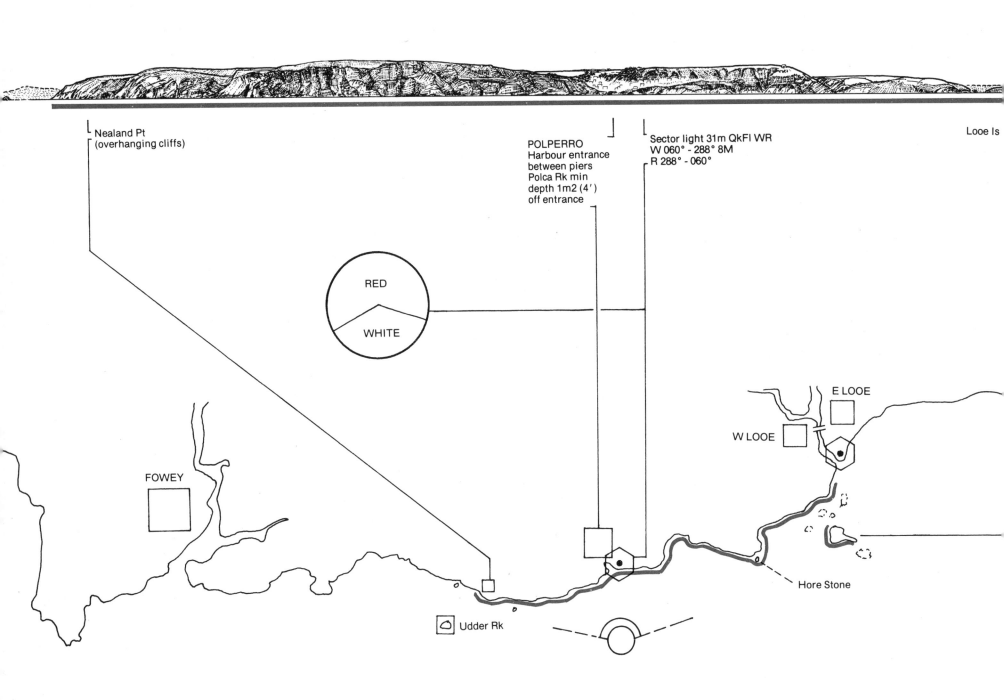

Nealand Pt
(overhanging cliffs)

POLPERRO
Harbour entrance
between piers
Polca Rk min
depth 1m2 (4′)
off entrance

Sector light 31m QkFl WR
W 060° - 288° 8M
R 288° - 060°

Looe Is

RED

WHITE

E LOOE

W LOOE

FOWEY

Hore Stone

Udder Rk

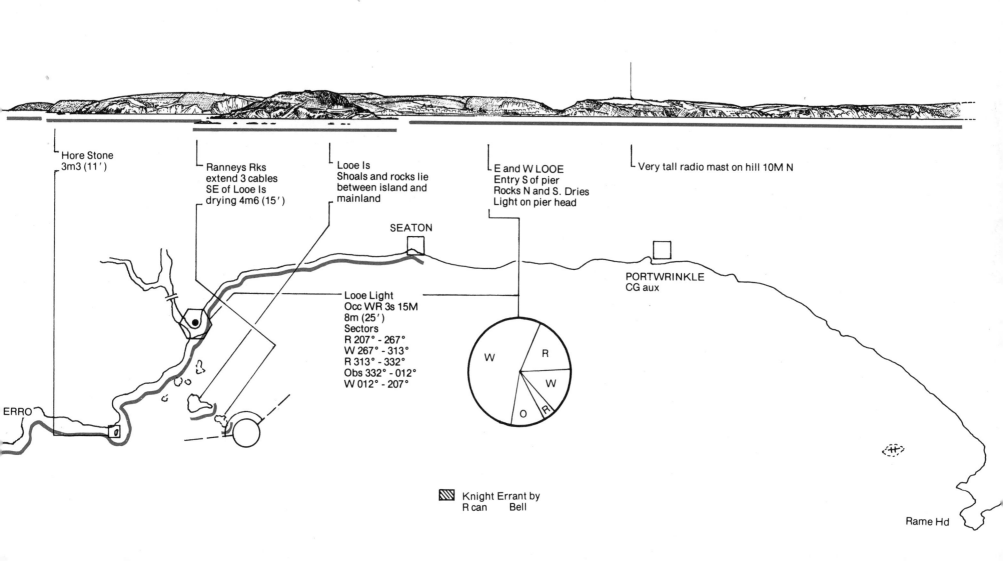

Hore Stone
3m3 (11′)

Ranneys Rks
extend 3 cables
SE of Looe Is
drying 4m6 (15′)

Looe Is
Shoals and rocks lie
between island and
mainland

E and W LOOE
Entry S of pier
Rocks N and S. Dries
Light on pier head

Very tall radio mast on hill 10M N

SEATON

Looe Light
Occ WR 3s 15M
8m (25′)
Sectors
R 207° - 267°
W 267° - 313°
R 313° - 332°
Obs 332° - 012°
W 012° - 207°

W   R

W

O   R

PORTWRINKLE
CG aux

ERRO

Knight Errant by
R can   Bell

Rame Hd

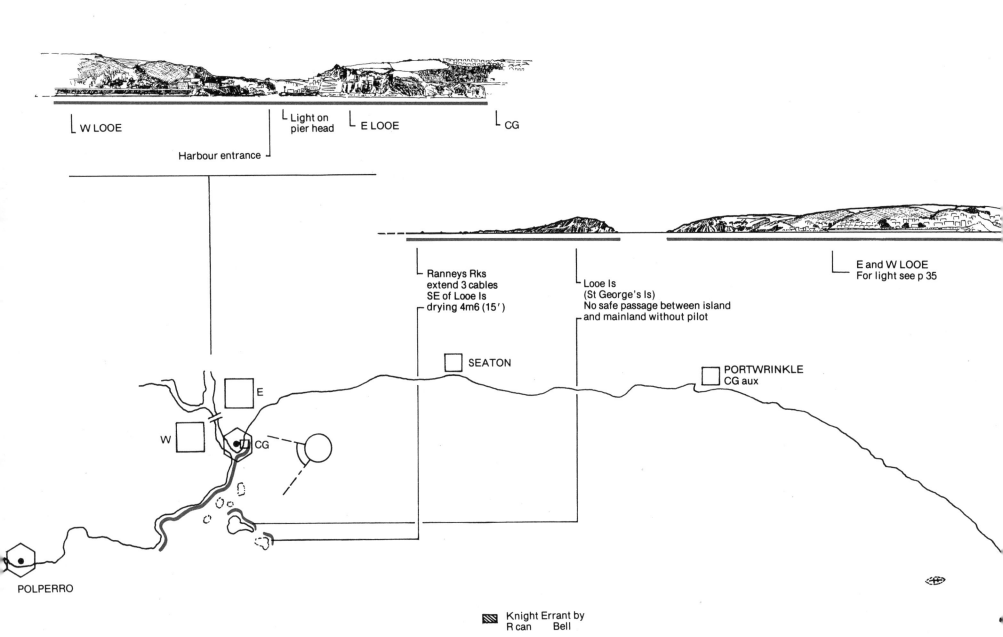

W LOOE   Light on pier head   E LOOE   CG

Harbour entrance

Ranneys Rks
extend 3 cables
SE of Looe Is
drying 4m6 (15′)

Looe Is
(St George's Is)
No safe passage between island
and mainland without pilot

E and W LOOE
For light see p 35

SEATON

PORTWRINKLE
CG aux

E

W

CG

POLPERRO

Knight Errant by
R can   Bell

Rame Hd

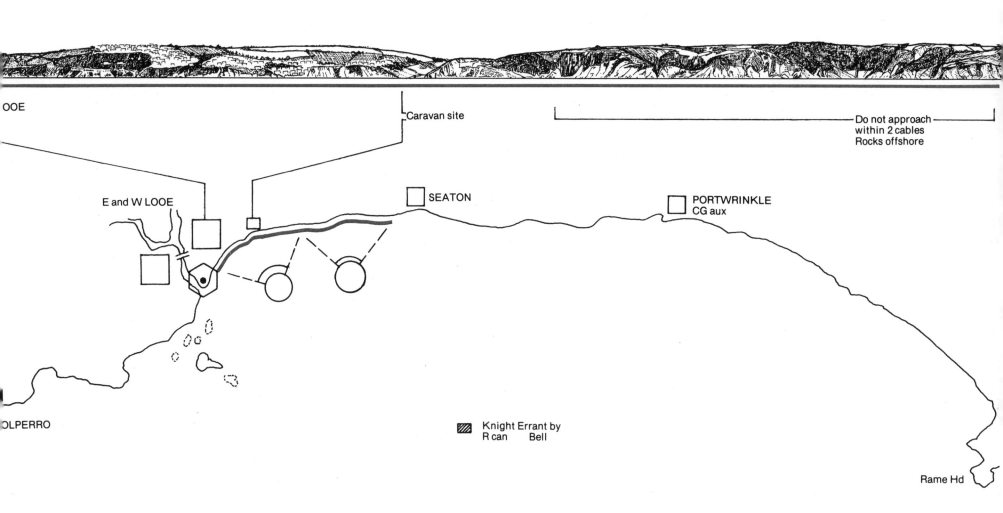

OOE

E and W LOOE

Caravan site

SEATON

PORTWRINKLE
CG aux

Do not approach
within 2 cables
Rocks offshore

OLPERRO

Knight Errant by
R can   Bell

Rame Hd

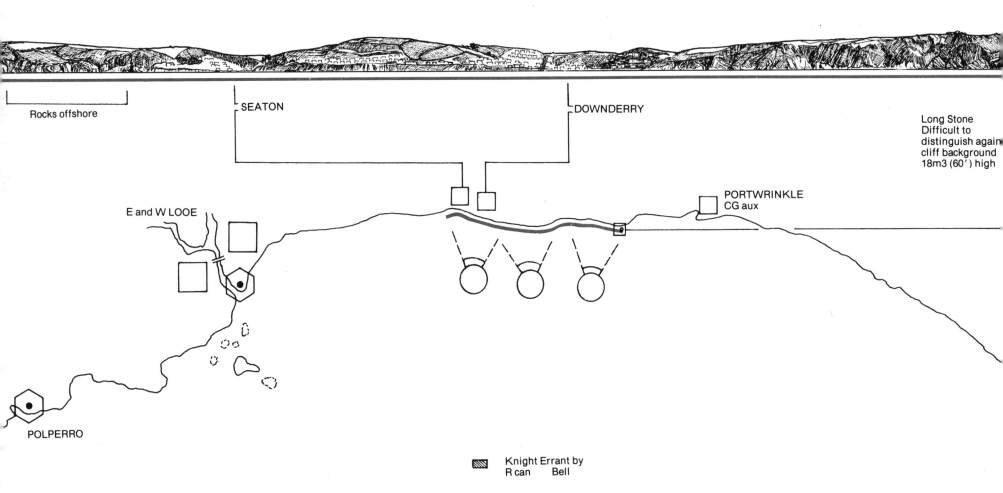

DANGER: Refer to chart before approaching within two
cables of shore. Many offlying rocks

Rocks offshore

SEATON

DOWNDERRY

Long Stone
Difficult to
distinguish again
cliff background
18m3 (60′) high

E and W LOOE

PORTWRINKLE
CG aux

POLPERRO

Knight Errant by
R can   Bell

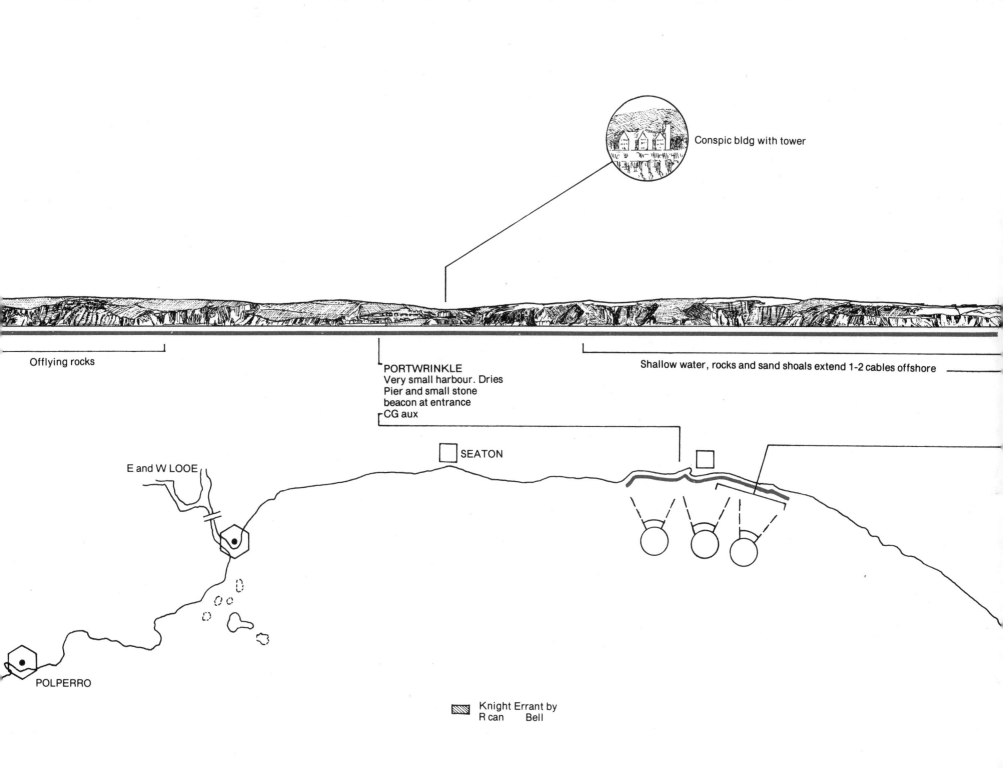

Conspic bldg with tower

Offlying rocks

PORTWRINKLE
Very small harbour. Dries
Pier and small stone
beacon at entrance
CG aux

Shallow water, rocks and sand shoals extend 1-2 cables offshore

E and W LOOE

SEATON

POLPERRO

Knight Errant by
R can   Bell

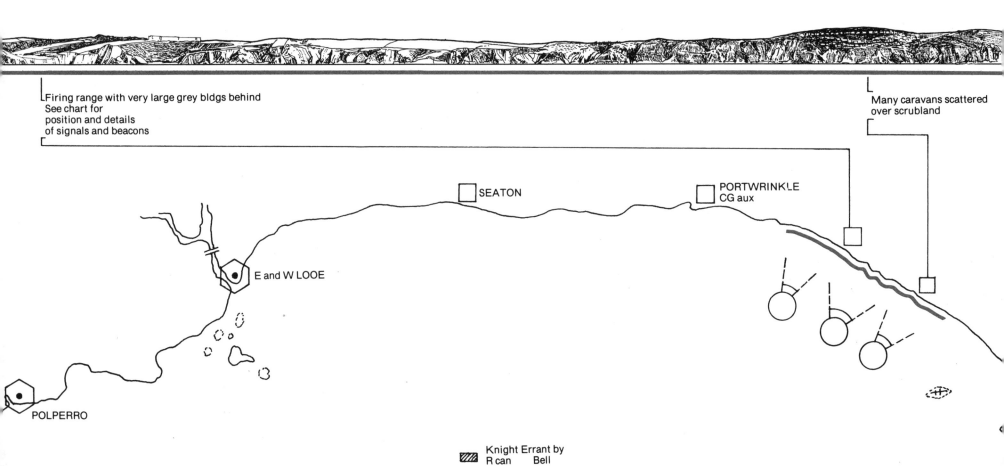

Firing range with very large grey bldgs behind
See chart for
position and details
of signals and beacons

Many caravans scattered
over scrubland

SEATON

PORTWRINKLE
CG aux

E and W LOOE

POLPERRO

Knight Errant by
R can   Bell

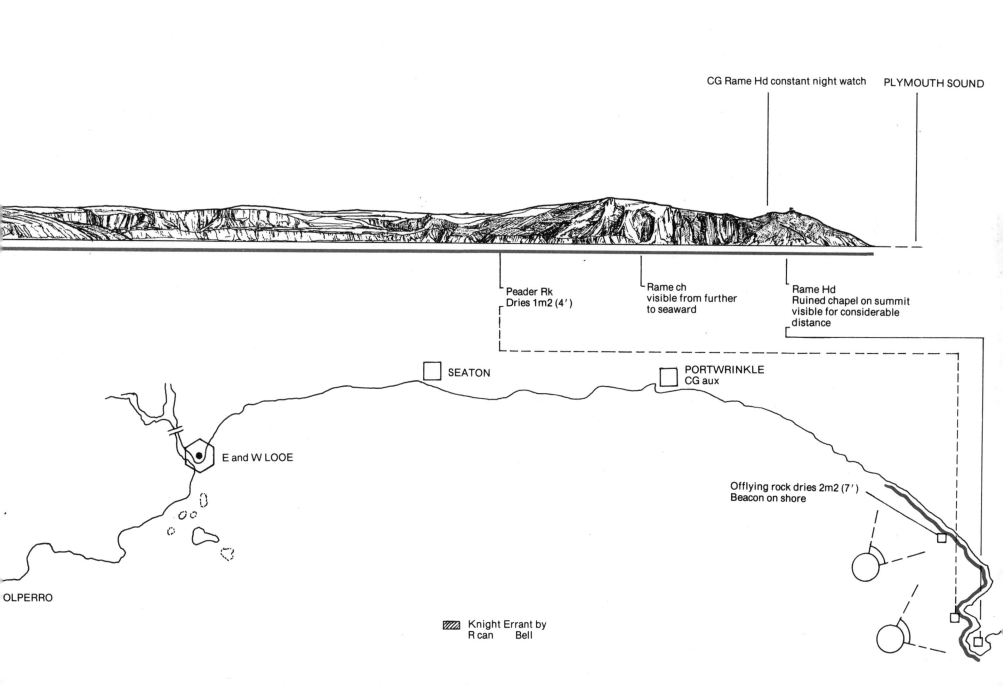

CG Rame Hd constant night watch   PLYMOUTH SOUND

Peader Rk
Dries 1m2 (4')

Rame ch
visible from further
to seaward

Rame Hd
Ruined chapel on summit
visible for considerable
distance

SEATON

PORTWRINKLE
CG aux

E and W LOOE

Offlying rock dries 2m2 (7')
Beacon on shore

OLPERRO

Knight Errant by
R can   Bell

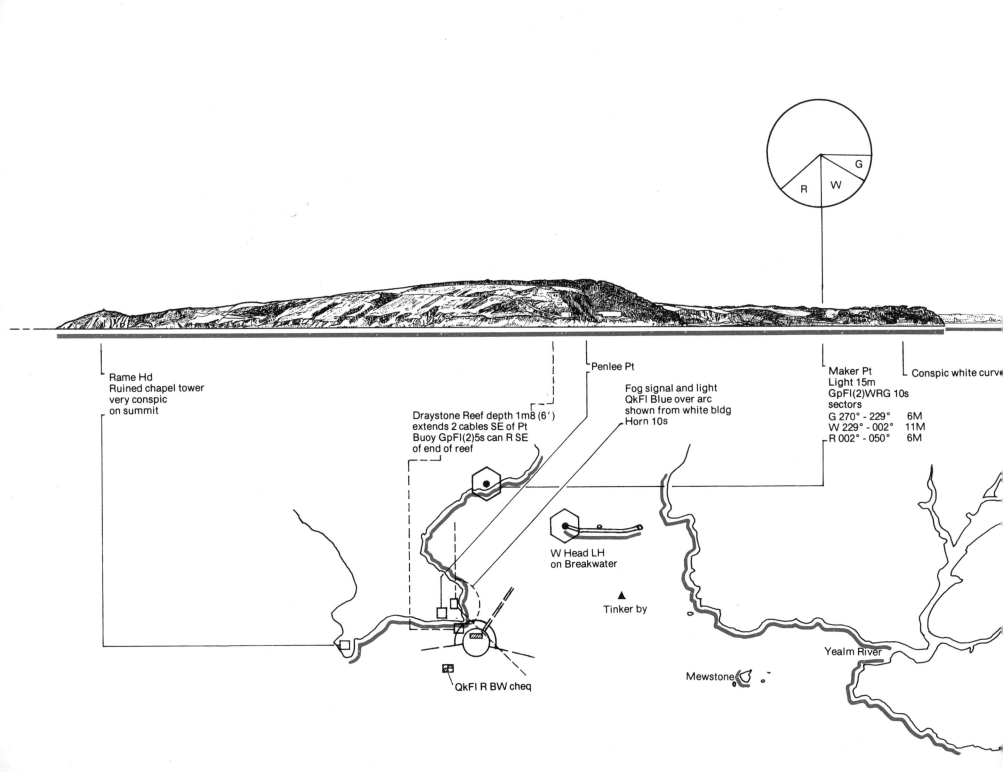

Rame Hd
Ruined chapel tower
very conspic
on summit

Penlee Pt

Fog signal and light
QkFl Blue over arc
shown from white bldg
Horn 10s

Maker Pt
Light 15m
GpFl(2)WRG 10s
sectors
G 270° - 229°   6M
W 229° - 002°   11M
R 002° - 050°   6M

Conspic white curve

Draystone Reef depth 1m8 (6′)
extends 2 cables SE of Pt
Buoy GpFl(2)5s can R SE
of end of reef

W Head LH
on Breakwater

R

W

G

Tinker by

Yealm River

QkFl R BW cheq

Mewstone

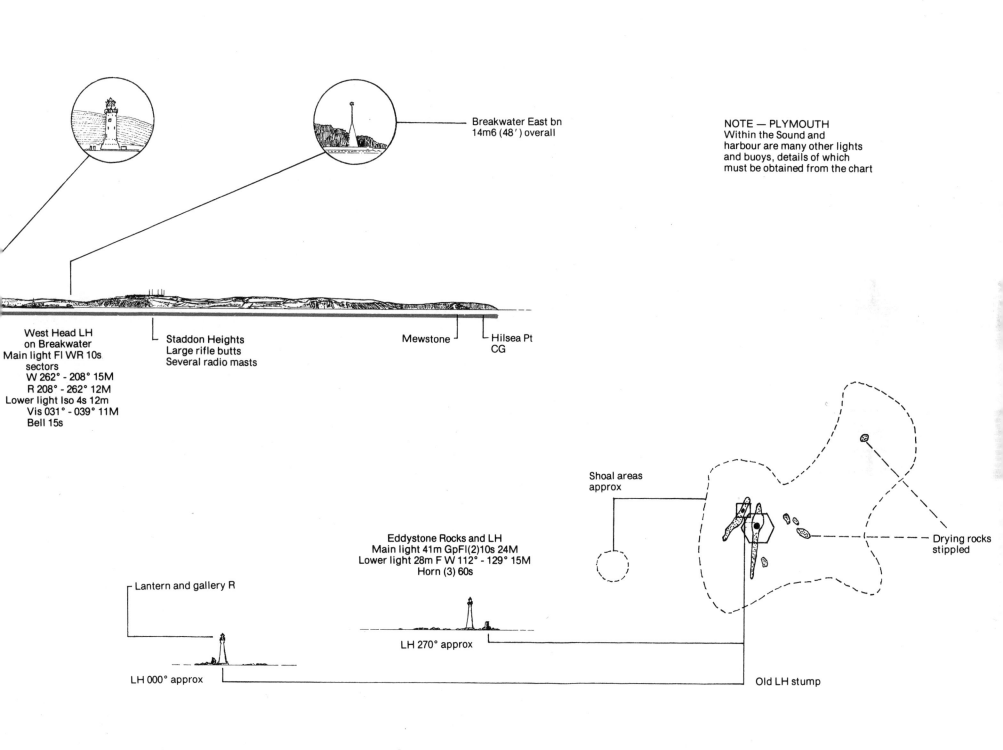

Breakwater East bn
14m6 (48') overall

NOTE — PLYMOUTH
Within the Sound and
harbour are many other lights
and buoys, details of which
must be obtained from the chart

West Head LH
on Breakwater
Main light Fl WR 10s
    sectors
    W 262° - 208° 15M
    R 208° - 262° 12M
Lower light Iso 4s 12m
    Vis 031° - 039° 11M
    Bell 15s

Staddon Heights
Large rifle butts
Several radio masts

Mewstone

Hilsea Pt
CG

Shoal areas
approx

Drying rocks
stippled

Eddystone Rocks and LH
Main light 41m GpFl(2)10s 24M
Lower light 28m F W 112° - 129° 15M
Horn (3) 60s

Lantern and gallery R

LH 270° approx

LH 000° approx

Old LH stump

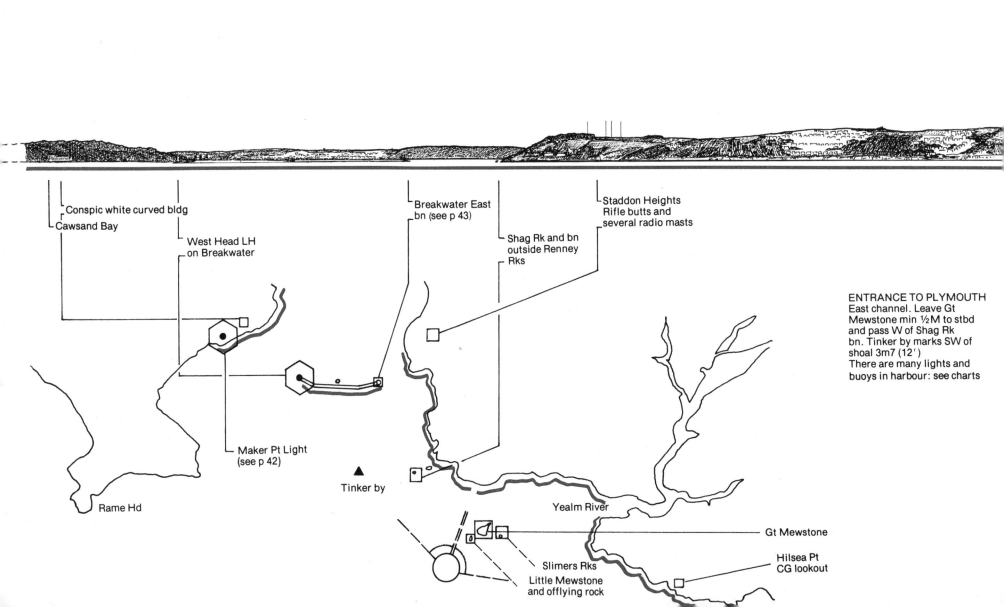

Conspic white curved bldg

Cawsand Bay

West Head LH
on Breakwater

Breakwater East
bn (see p 43)

Staddon Heights
Rifle butts and
several radio masts

Shag Rk and bn
outside Renney
Rks

ENTRANCE TO PLYMOUTH
East channel. Leave Gt
Mewstone min ½M to stbd
and pass W of Shag Rk
bn. Tinker by marks SW of
shoal 3m7 (12′)
There are many lights and
buoys in harbour: see charts

Maker Pt Light
(see p 42)

Tinker by

Rame Hd

Yealm River

Gt Mewstone

Slimers Rks

Little Mewstone
and offlying rock

Hilsea Pt
CG lookout

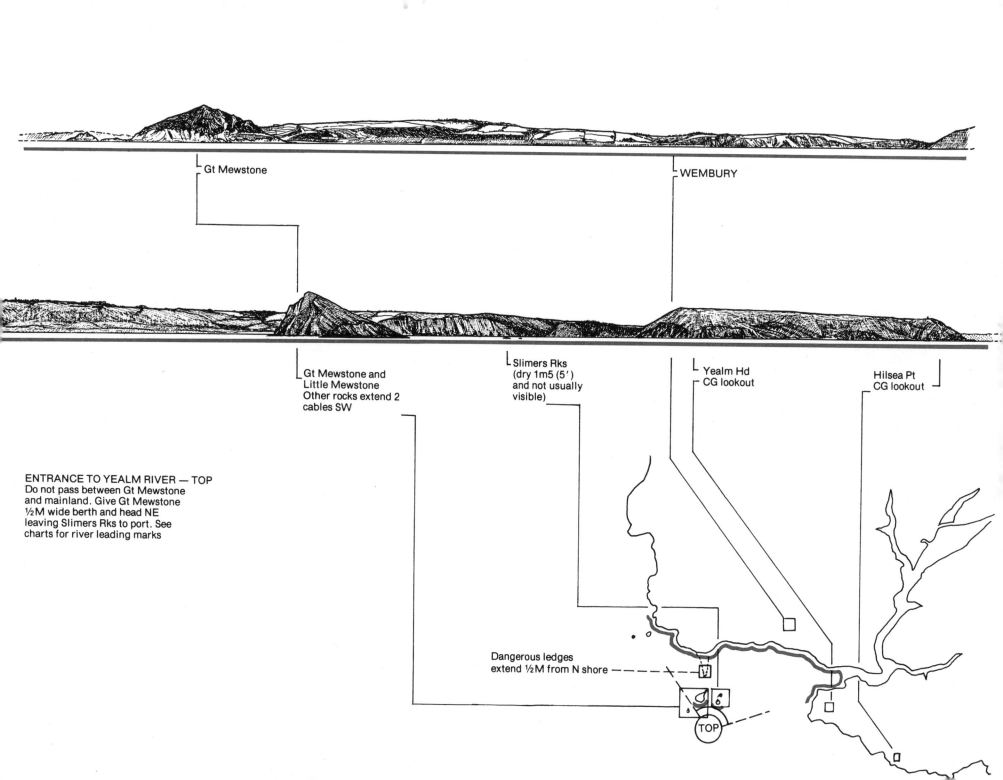

Gt Mewstone

WEMBURY

Gt Mewstone and
Little Mewstone
Other rocks extend 2
cables SW

Slimers Rks
(dry 1m5 (5′)
and not usually
visible)

Yealm Hd
CG lookout

Hilsea Pt
CG lookout

ENTRANCE TO YEALM RIVER — TOP
Do not pass between Gt Mewstone
and mainland. Give Gt Mewstone
½M wide berth and head NE
leaving Slimers Rks to port. See
charts for river leading marks

Dangerous ledges
extend ½M from N shore

TOP

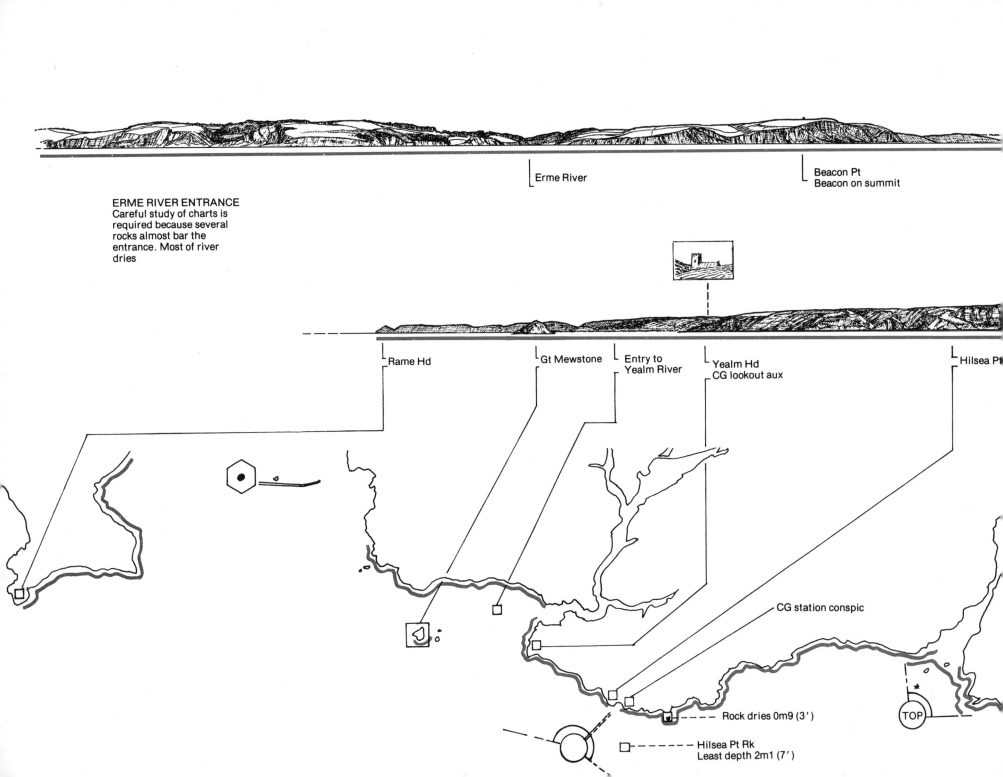

Erme River

Beacon Pt
Beacon on summit

ERME RIVER ENTRANCE
Careful study of charts is
required because several
rocks almost bar the
entrance. Most of river
dries

Rame Hd

Gt Mewstone

Entry to
Yealm River

Yealm Hd
CG lookout aux

Hilsea P

CG station conspic

Rock dries 0m9 (3')

TOP

Hilsea Pt Rk
Least depth 2m1 (7')

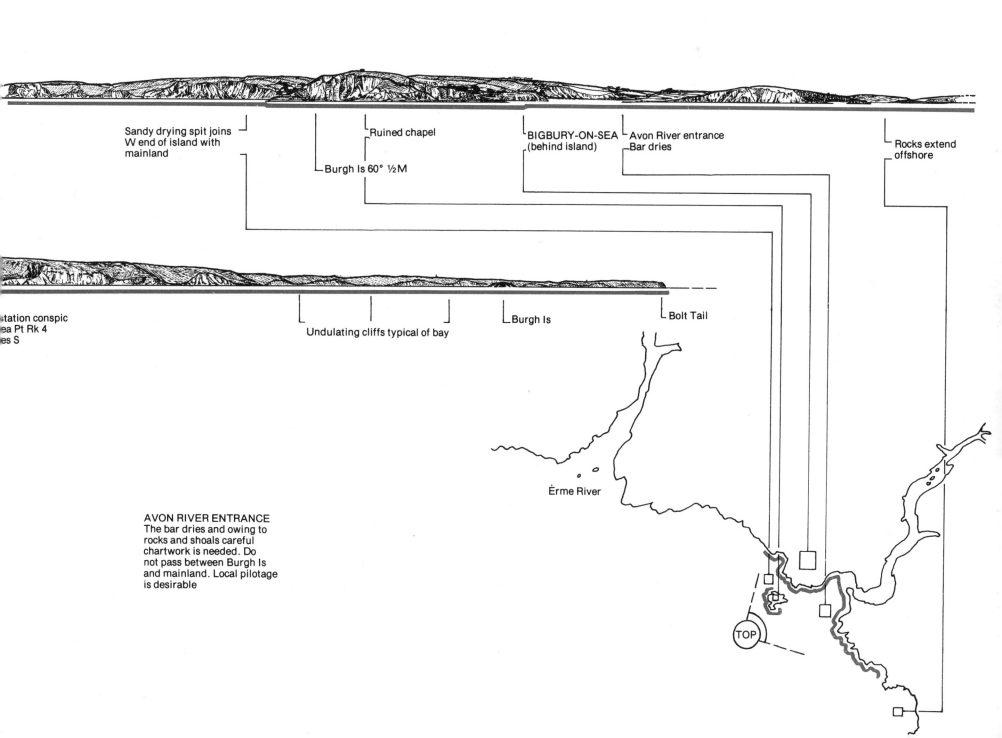

Sandy drying spit joins
W end of island with
mainland

Ruined chapel

Burgh Is 60° ½M

BIGBURY-ON-SEA
(behind island)

Avon River entrance
Bar dries

Rocks extend
offshore

station conspic
ea Pt Rk 4
es S

Undulating cliffs typical of bay

Burgh Is

Bolt Tail

Erme River

AVON RIVER ENTRANCE
The bar dries and owing to
rocks and shoals careful
chartwork is needed. Do
not pass between Burgh Is
and mainland. Local pilotage
is desirable

TOP

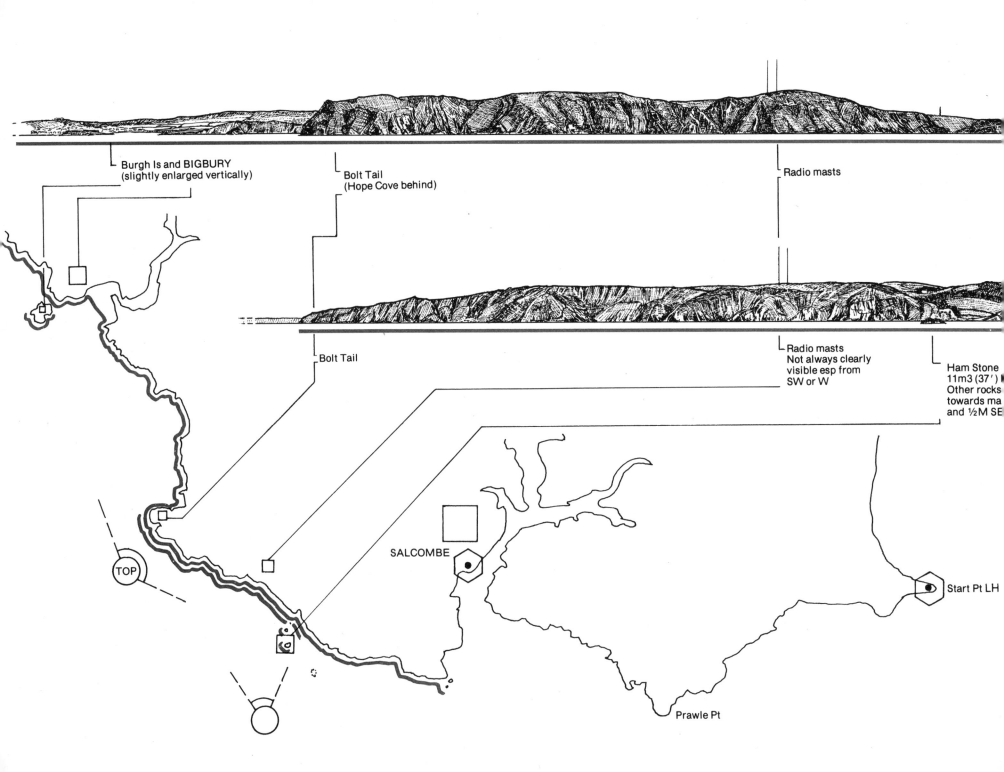

Burgh Is and BIGBURY
(slightly enlarged vertically)

Bolt Tail
(Hope Cove behind)

Radio masts

Bolt Tail

Radio masts
Not always clearly
visible esp from
SW or W

Ham Stone
11m3 (37')
Other rocks
towards ma
and ½M SE

SALCOMBE

TOP

Start Pt LH

Prawle Pt

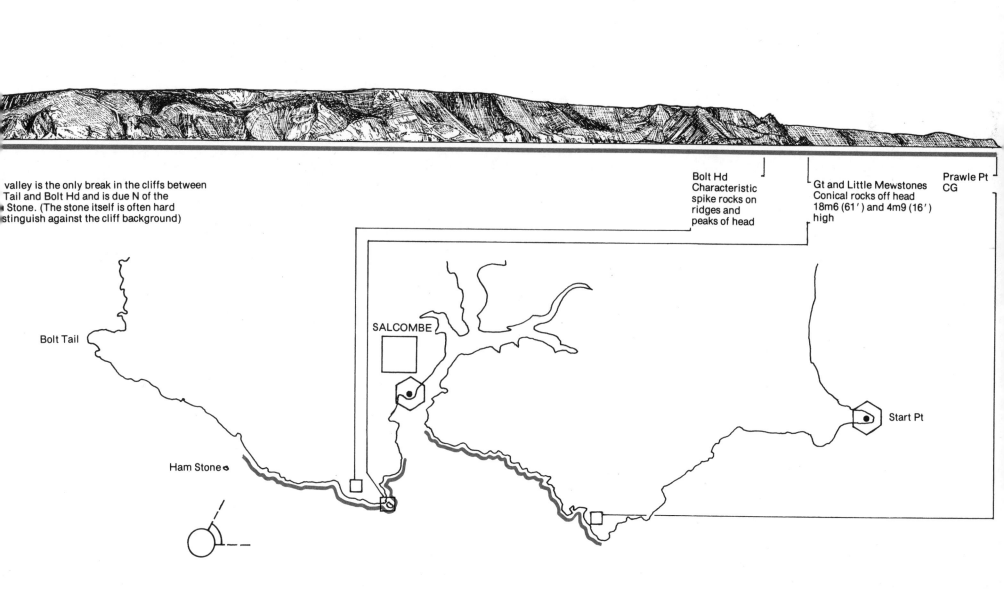

valley is the only break in the cliffs between
Tail and Bolt Hd and is due N of the
Stone. (The stone itself is often hard
stinguish against the cliff background)

Bolt Hd
Characteristic
spike rocks on
ridges and
peaks of head

Gt and Little Mewstones
Conical rocks off head
18m6 (61′) and 4m9 (16′)
high

Prawle Pt
CG

Bolt Tail

SALCOMBE

Ham Stone

Start Pt

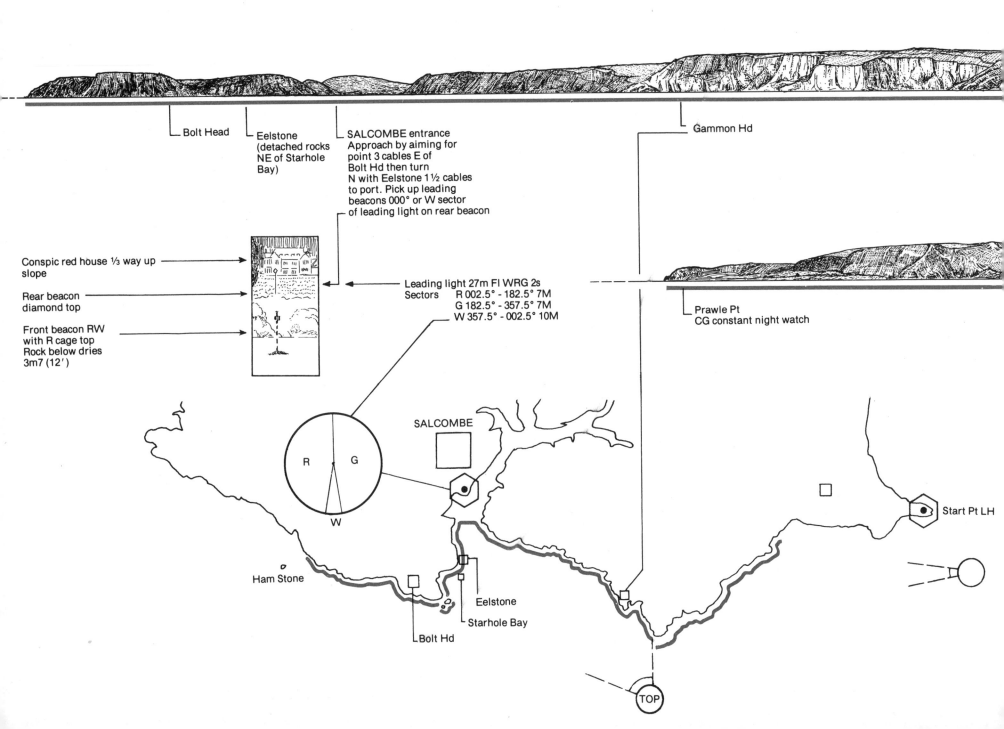

Bolt Head

Eelstone
(detached rocks
NE of Starhole
Bay)

SALCOMBE entrance
Approach by aiming for
point 3 cables E of
Bolt Hd then turn
N with Eelstone 1½ cables
to port. Pick up leading
beacons 000° or W sector
of leading light on rear beacon

Gammon Hd

Conspic red house ⅓ way up
slope

Rear beacon
diamond top

Front beacon RW
with R cage top
Rock below dries
3m7 (12')

Leading light 27m Fl WRG 2s
Sectors   R 002.5° - 182.5° 7M
           G 182.5° - 357.5° 7M
           W 357.5° - 002.5° 10M

Prawle Pt
CG constant night watch

SALCOMBE

R   G

W

Start Pt LH

Ham Stone

Eelstone

Starhole Bay

Bolt Hd

TOP

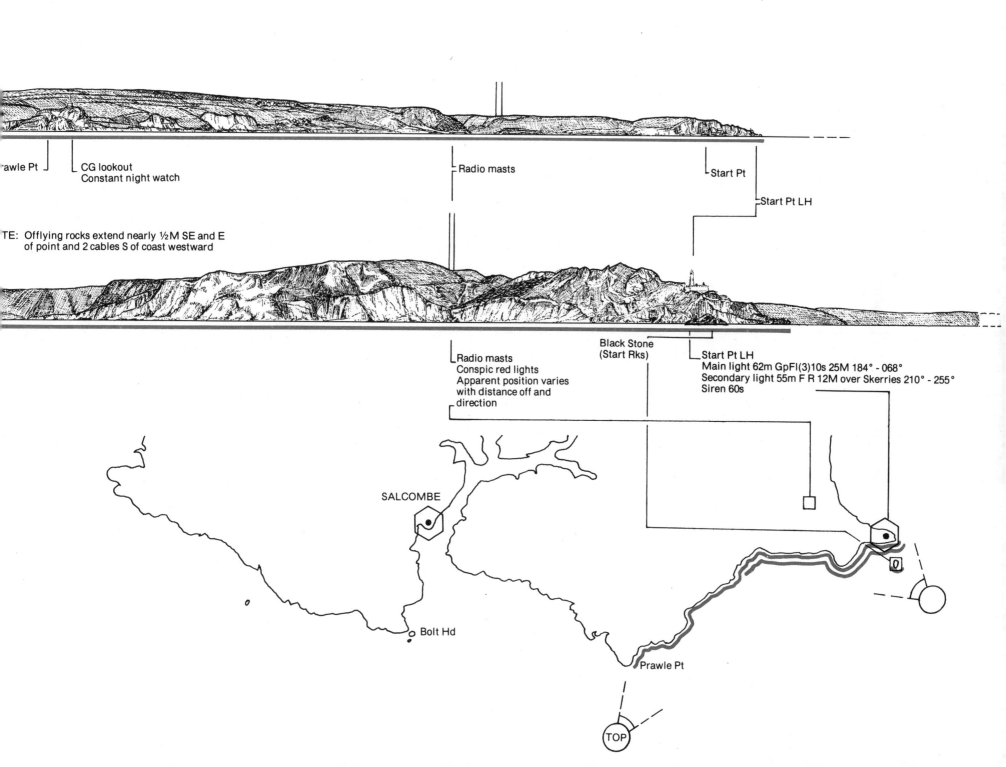

rawle Pt   CG lookout
            Constant night watch

Radio masts

Start Pt

Start Pt LH

TE: Offlying rocks extend nearly ½M SE and E
    of point and 2 cables S of coast westward

Radio masts
Conspic red lights
Apparent position varies
with distance off and
direction

Black Stone
(Start Rks)

Start Pt LH
Main light 62m GpFl(3)10s 25M 184° - 068°
Secondary light 55m F R 12M over Skerries 210° - 255°
Siren 60s

SALCOMBE

Bolt Hd

Prawle Pt

TOP

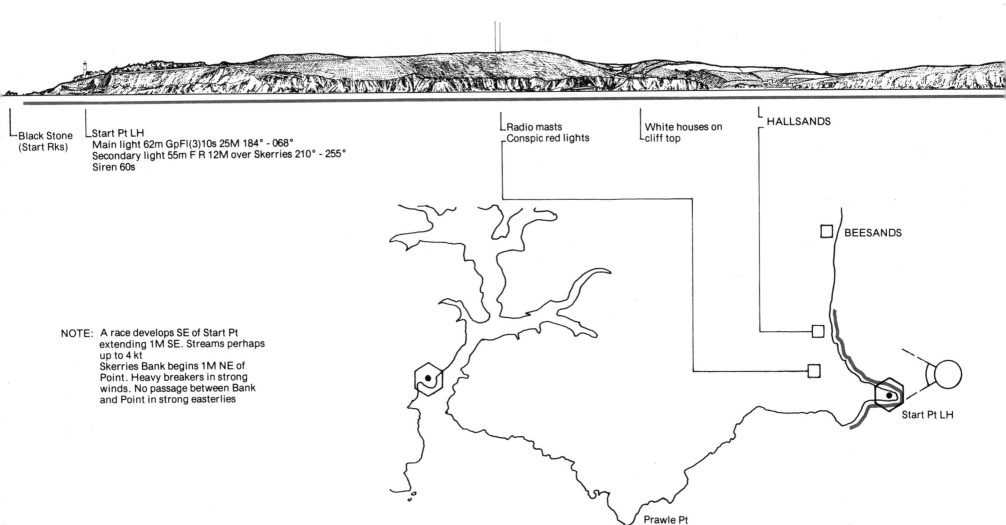

Black Stone
(Start Rks)

Start Pt LH
Main light 62m GpFl(3)10s 25M 184° - 068°
Secondary light 55m F R 12M over Skerries 210° - 255°
Siren 60s

Radio masts
Conspic red lights

White houses on
cliff top

HALLSANDS

BEESANDS

Start Pt LH

Prawle Pt

NOTE: A race develops SE of Start Pt
extending 1M SE. Streams perhaps
up to 4 kt
Skerries Bank begins 1M NE of
Point. Heavy breakers in strong
winds. No passage between Bank
and Point in strong easterlies

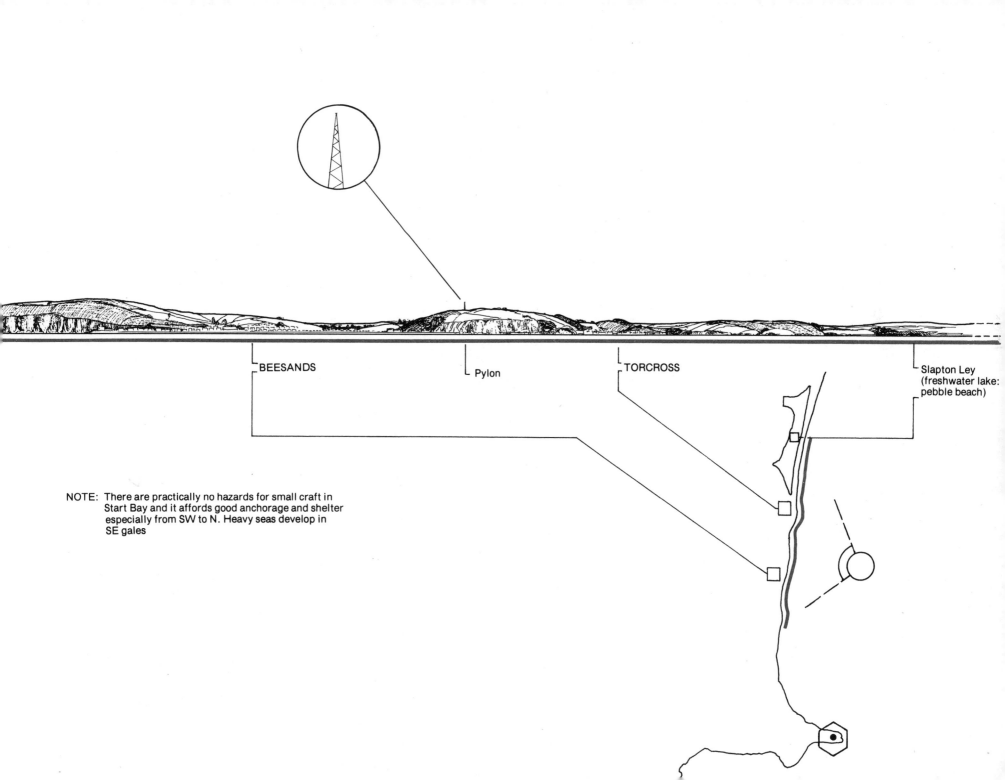

BEESANDS

Pylon

TORCROSS

Slapton Ley
(freshwater lake:
pebble beach)

NOTE: There are practically no hazards for small craft in
Start Bay and it affords good anchorage and shelter
especially from SW to N. Heavy seas develop in
SE gales

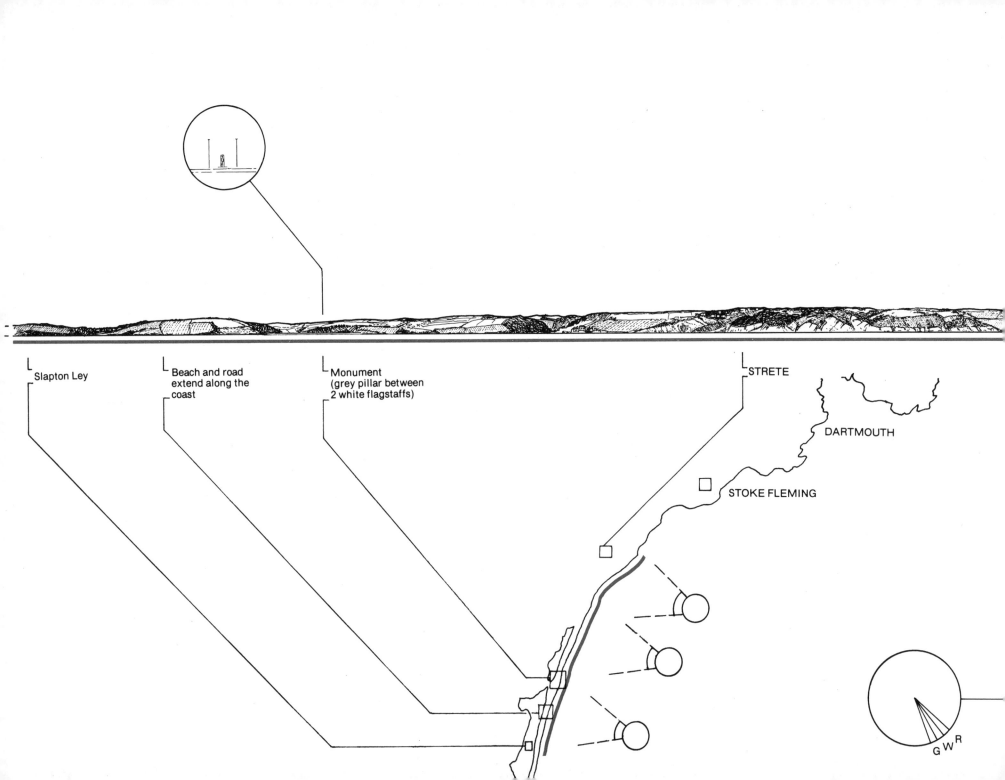

Slapton Ley

Beach and road
extend along the
coast

Monument
(grey pillar between
2 white flagstaffs)

STRETE

DARTMOUTH

STOKE FLEMING

G W R

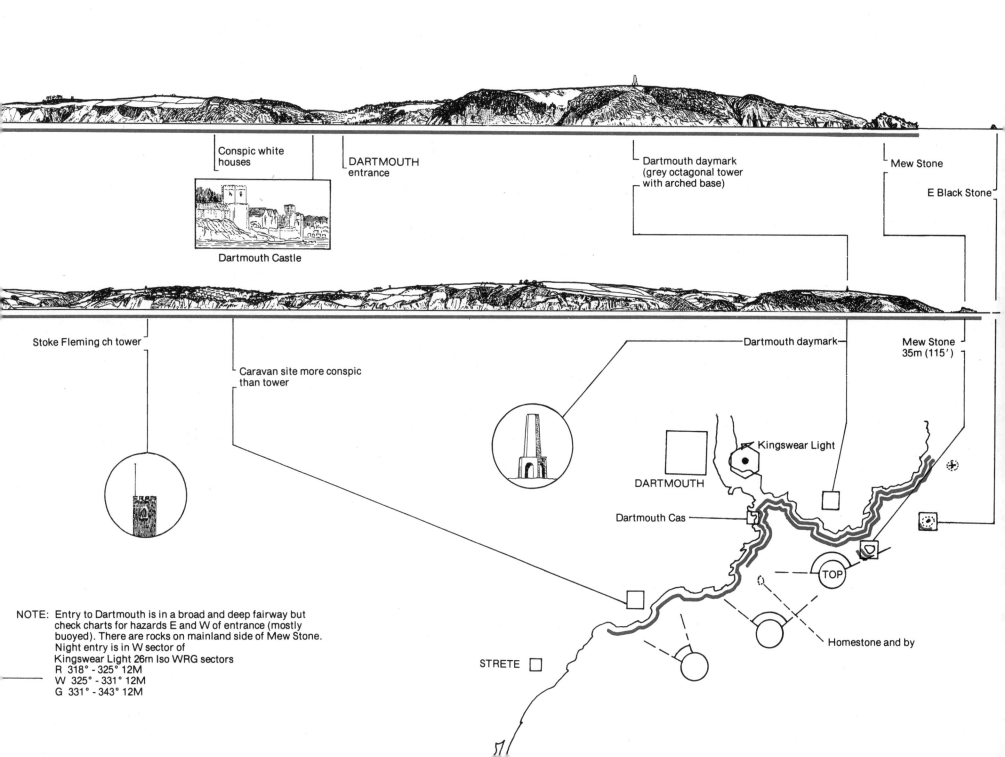

Conspic white houses

DARTMOUTH entrance

Dartmouth daymark (grey octagonal tower with arched base)

Mew Stone

E Black Stone

Dartmouth Castle

Stoke Fleming ch tower

Caravan site more conspic than tower

Dartmouth daymark

Mew Stone 35m (115')

Kingswear Light

DARTMOUTH

Dartmouth Cas

TOP

Homestone and by

STRETE

NOTE: Entry to Dartmouth is in a broad and deep fairway but check charts for hazards E and W of entrance (mostly buoyed). There are rocks on mainland side of Mew Stone. Night entry is in W sector of Kingswear Light 26m Iso WRG sectors
R 318° - 325° 12M
W 325° - 331° 12M
G 331° - 343° 12M

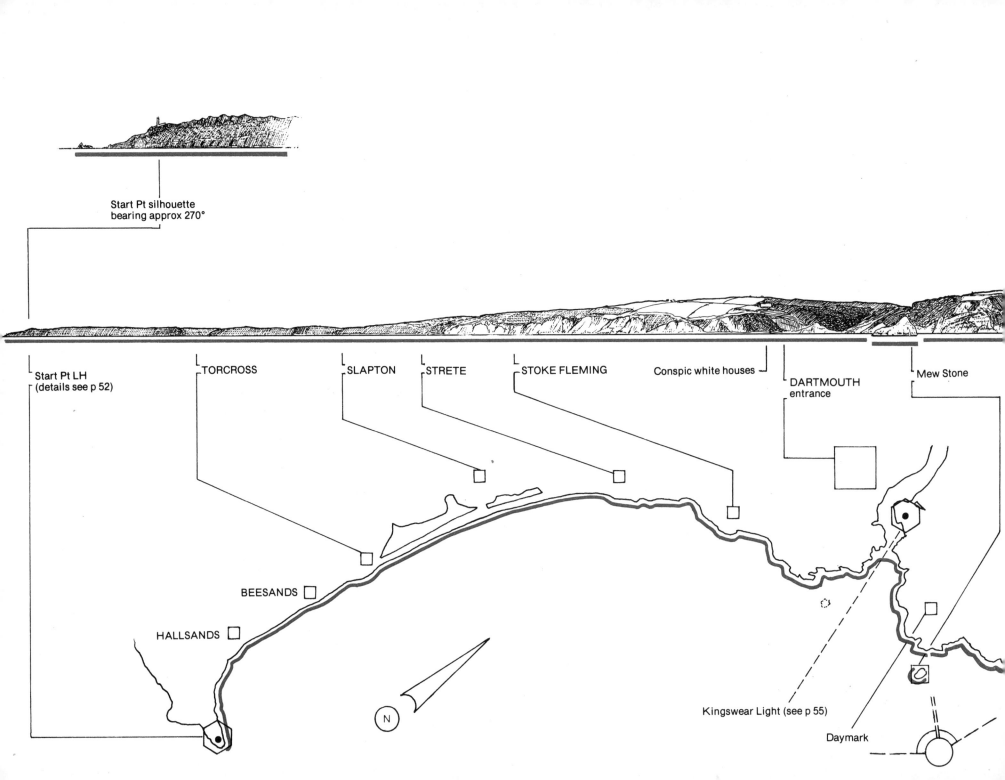

Start Pt silhouette
bearing approx 270°

Start Pt LH
(details see p 52)

TORCROSS

SLAPTON

STRETE

STOKE FLEMING

Conspic white houses

DARTMOUTH
entrance

Mew Stone

BEESANDS

HALLSANDS

N

Kingswear Light (see p 55)

Daymark

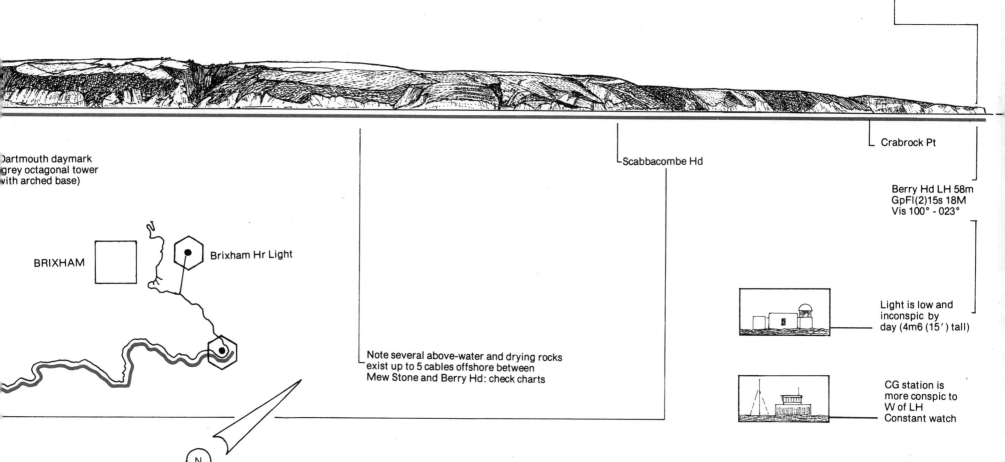

Berry Hd approx 000°
Cod Rk vis off
head from further W

Crabrock Pt

Scabbacombe Hd

Dartmouth daymark
(grey octagonal tower
with arched base)

Berry Hd LH 58m
GpFl(2)15s 18M
Vis 100° - 023°

BRIXHAM   Brixham Hr Light

Light is low and
inconspic by
day (4m6 (15') tall)

Note several above-water and drying rocks
exist up to 5 cables offshore between
Mew Stone and Berry Hd: check charts

CG station is
more conspic to
W of LH
Constant watch

N

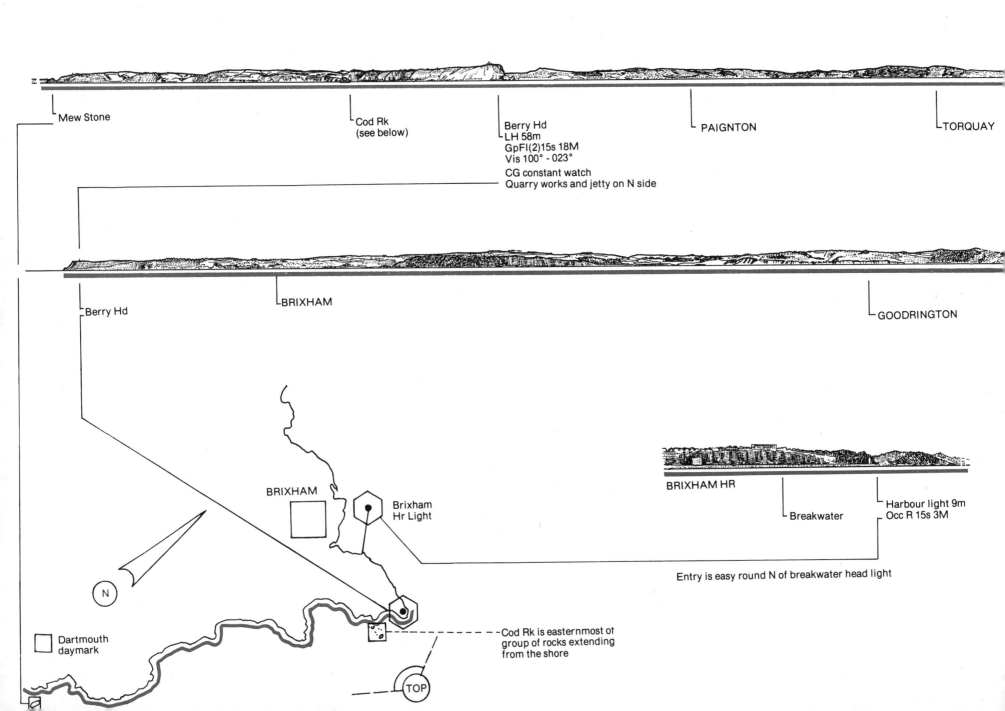

Mew Stone

Cod Rk
(see below)

Berry Hd
LH 58m
GpFl(2)15s 18M
Vis 100° - 023°
CG constant watch
Quarry works and jetty on N side

PAIGNTON

TORQUAY

Berry Hd

BRIXHAM

GOODRINGTON

BRIXHAM HR

BRIXHAM

Brixham
Hr Light

Breakwater

Harbour light 9m
Occ R 15s 3M

Entry is easy round N of breakwater head light

N

Dartmouth
daymark

Cod Rk is easternmost of
group of rocks extending
from the shore

TOP

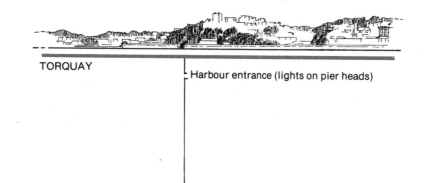

TORQUAY

⌐ Harbour entrance (lights on pier heads)

PAIGNTON
Small drying harbour between
Roundham Hd (red stone
headland) and East Pier.
Beacon to E of pier marks
spit end

⌐TORQUAY

Torquay Hr entrance
⌐ Easy, between pier heads
  Lights F R to port on entry
          F G to stbd on entry
⌐ Summer light buoy on approach

⌐ Conspic bldg

Thatcher Rk
⌐40m8 (134′)

⌐Ore Stone
⌐32m3 (106′) high

NOTE: Torbay is free of all hazards
       except shoal water near coastline
       and offlying rocks N of Berry Hd
       and between Torquay Hr and Ore Stone

PAIGNTON

TORQUAY

BRIXHAM

Shag Rks

N

Berry Hd LH

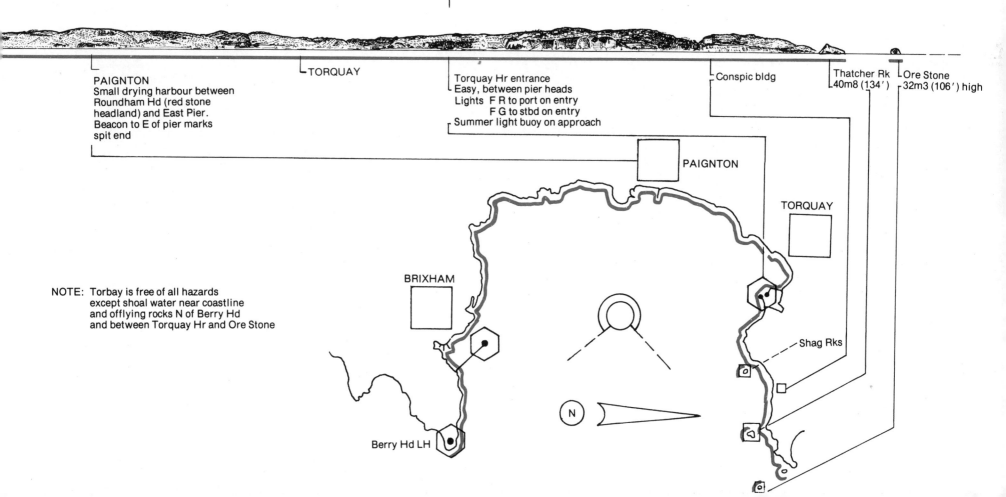

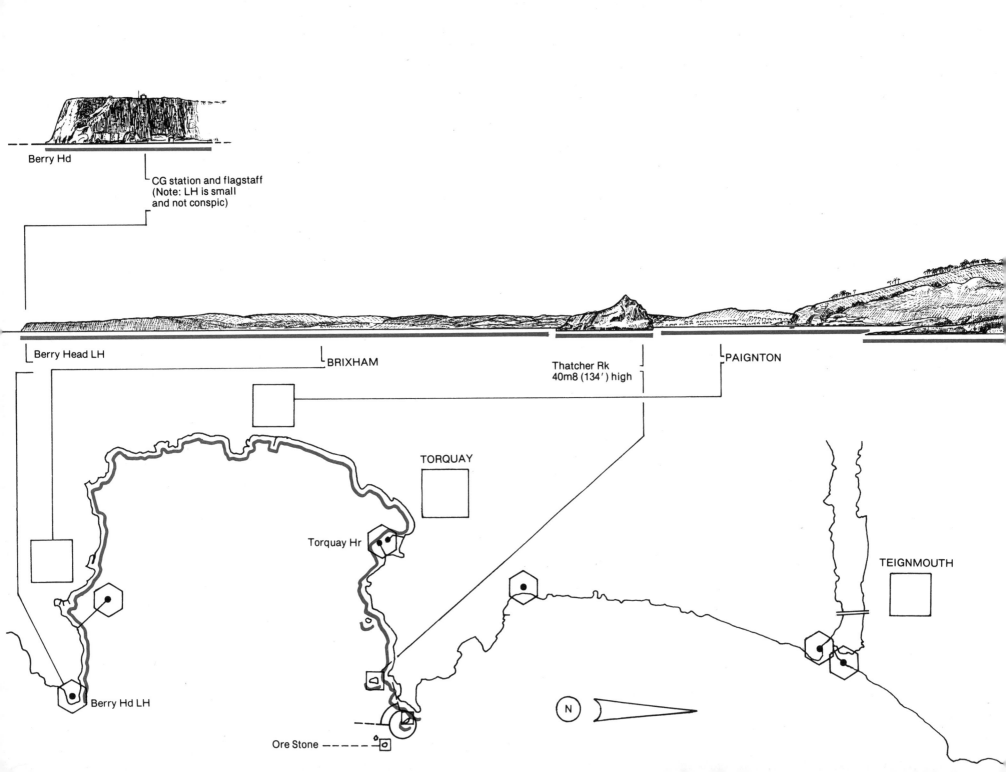

Berry Hd

CG station and flagstaff
(Note: LH is small
and not conspic)

Berry Head LH

BRIXHAM

Thatcher Rk
40m8 (134') high

PAIGNTON

TORQUAY

Torquay Hr

TEIGNMOUTH

Berry Hd LH

N

Ore Stone

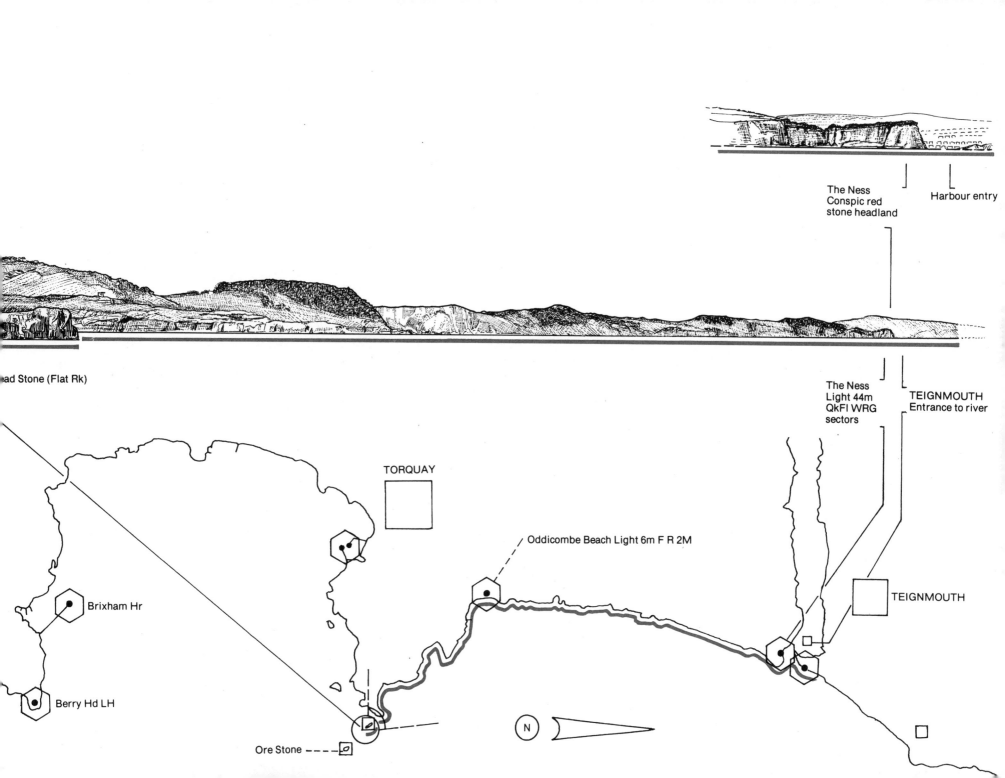

The Ness
Conspic red
stone headland

Harbour entry

ad Stone (Flat Rk)

The Ness
Light 44m
QkFl WRG
sectors

TEIGNMOUTH
Entrance to river

TORQUAY

Oddicombe Beach Light 6m F R 2M

Brixham Hr

TEIGNMOUTH

Berry Hd LH

N

Ore Stone

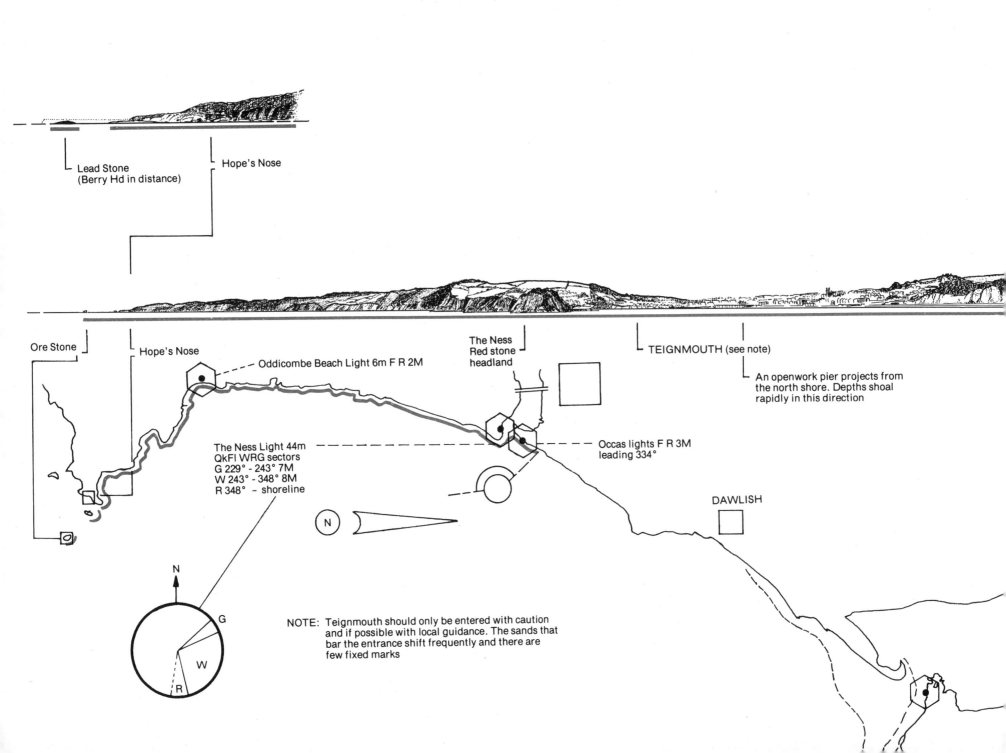

Lead Stone
(Berry Hd in distance)

Hope's Nose

Ore Stone

Hope's Nose

Oddicombe Beach Light 6m F R 2M

The Ness
Red stone
headland

TEIGNMOUTH (see note)

An openwork pier projects from
the north shore. Depths shoal
rapidly in this direction

The Ness Light 44m
QkFl WRG sectors
G 229° - 243° 7M
W 243° - 348° 8M
R 348° – shoreline

Occas lights F R 3M
leading 334°

N

DAWLISH

N

G

W

R

NOTE: Teignmouth should only be entered with caution
and if possible with local guidance. The sands that
bar the entrance shift frequently and there are
few fixed marks

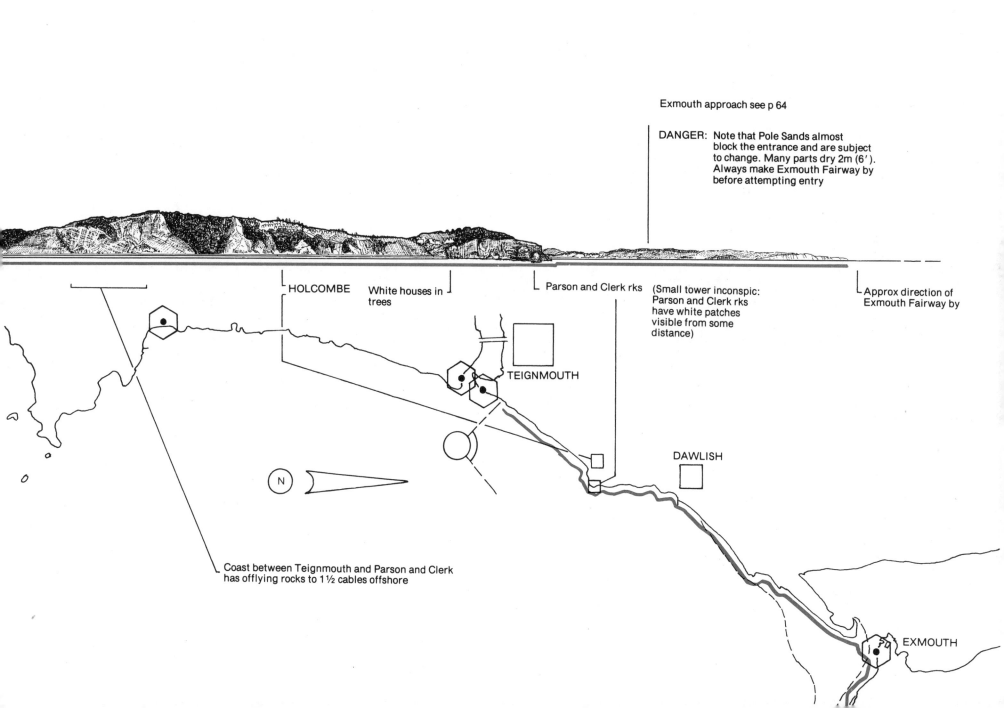

Exmouth approach see p 64

DANGER: Note that Pole Sands almost block the entrance and are subject to change. Many parts dry 2m (6'). Always make Exmouth Fairway by before attempting entry

HOLCOMBE

White houses in trees

Parson and Clerk rks

(Small tower inconspic: Parson and Clerk rks have white patches visible from some distance)

Approx direction of Exmouth Fairway by

TEIGNMOUTH

N

DAWLISH

Coast between Teignmouth and Parson and Clerk has offlying rocks to 1½ cables offshore

EXMOUTH

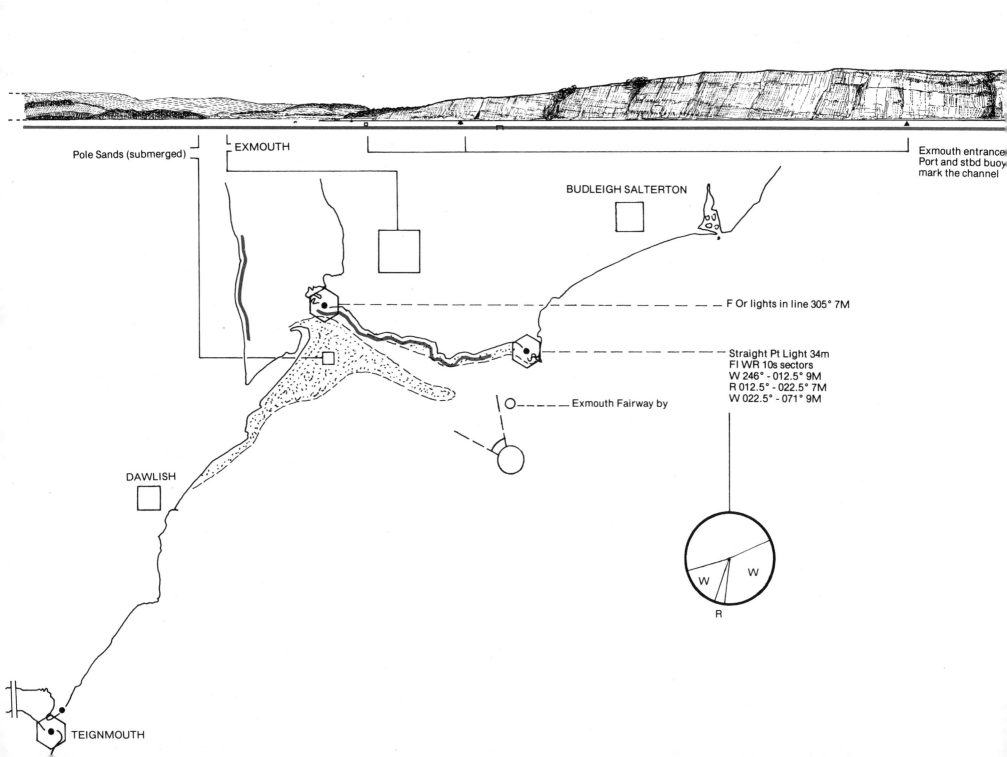

Pole Sands (submerged)

EXMOUTH

Exmouth entrance
Port and stbd buoy
mark the channel

BUDLEIGH SALTERTON

F Or lights in line 305° 7M

Straight Pt Light 34m
Fl WR 10s sectors
W 246° - 012.5° 9M
R 012.5° - 022.5° 7M
W 022.5° - 071° 9M

Exmouth Fairway by

W   W

R

DAWLISH

TEIGNMOUTH

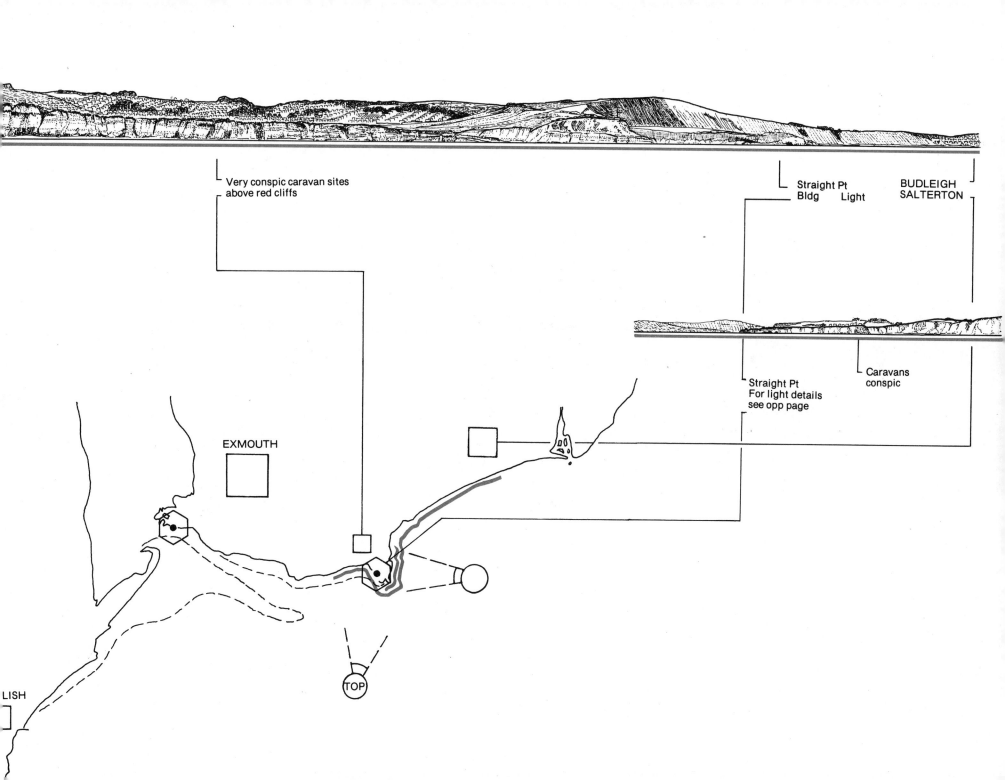

Very conspic caravan sites
above red cliffs

Straight Pt
Bldg   Light

BUDLEIGH
SALTERTON

Caravans
conspic

Straight Pt
For light details
see opp page

EXMOUTH

TOP

LISH

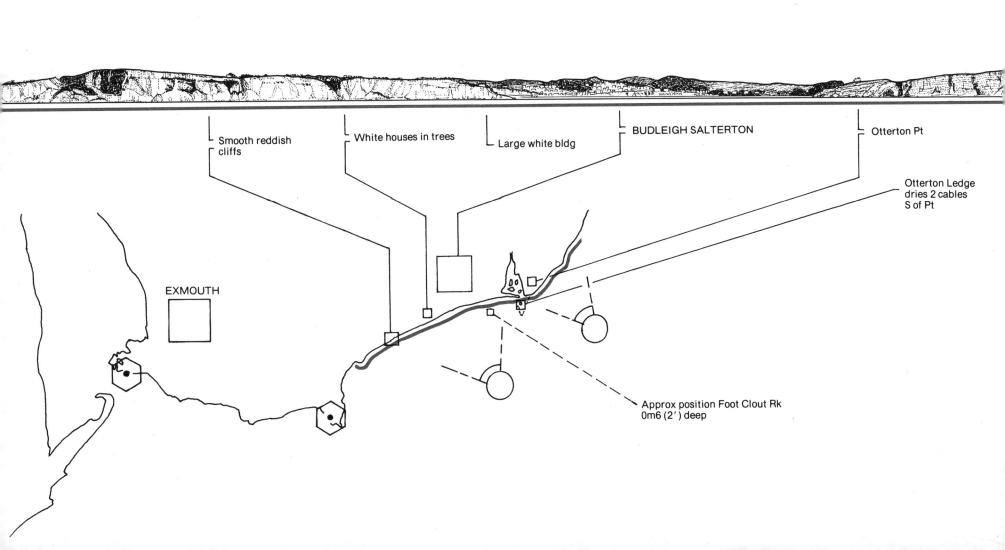

Smooth reddish cliffs

White houses in trees

Large white bldg

BUDLEIGH SALTERTON

Otterton Pt

Otterton Ledge
dries 2 cables
S of Pt

EXMOUTH

Approx position Foot Clout Rk
0m6 (2′) deep

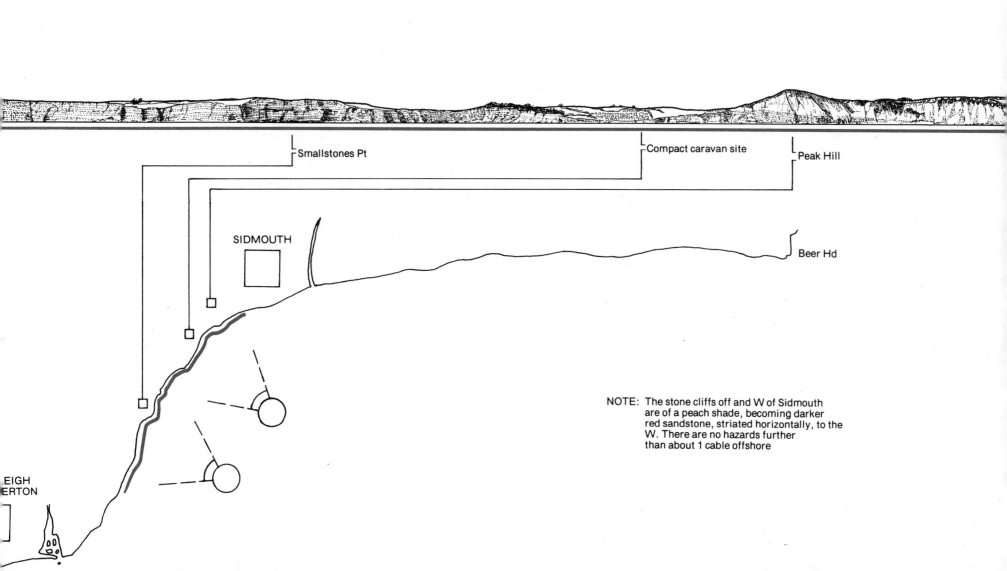

Smallstones Pt

Compact caravan site

Peak Hill

SIDMOUTH

Beer Hd

EIGH
ERTON

NOTE: The stone cliffs off and W of Sidmouth
are of a peach shade, becoming darker
red sandstone, striated horizontally, to the
W. There are no hazards further
than about 1 cable offshore

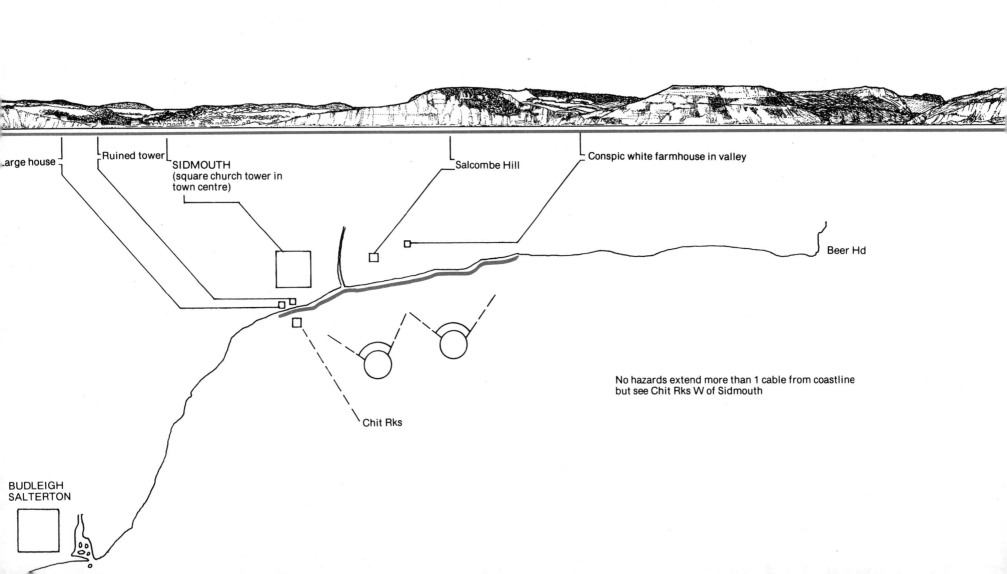

Large house

Ruined tower

SIDMOUTH
(square church tower in
town centre)

Salcombe Hill

Conspic white farmhouse in valley

Beer Hd

No hazards extend more than 1 cable from coastline
but see Chit Rks W of Sidmouth

Chit Rks

BUDLEIGH
SALTERTON

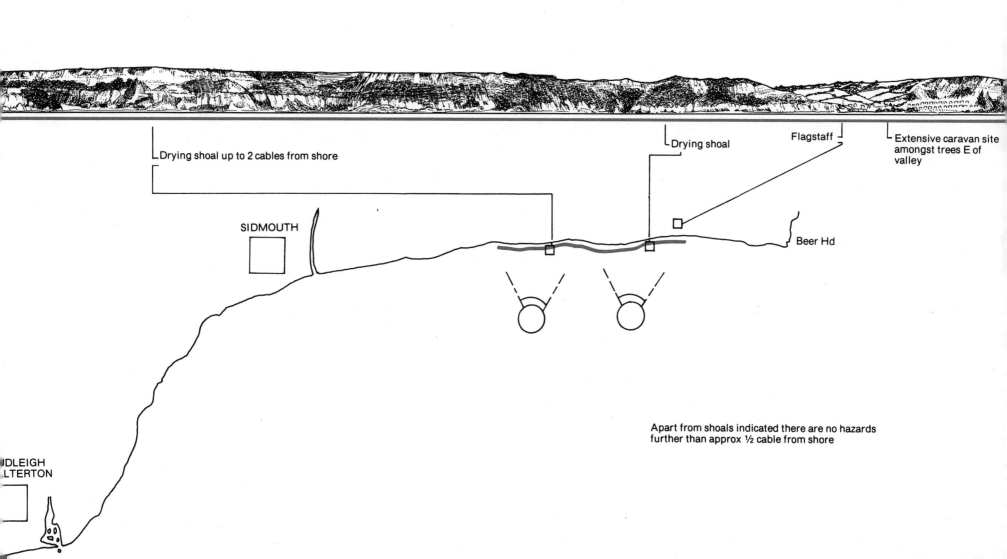

Drying shoal up to 2 cables from shore

Drying shoal

Flagstaff

Extensive caravan site amongst trees E of valley

SIDMOUTH

Beer Hd

Apart from shoals indicated there are no hazards further than approx ½ cable from shore

DLEIGH
LTERTON

Beer Hd from E

Very conspic caravan park
(lozenge-shaped) visible
from several miles in
sun

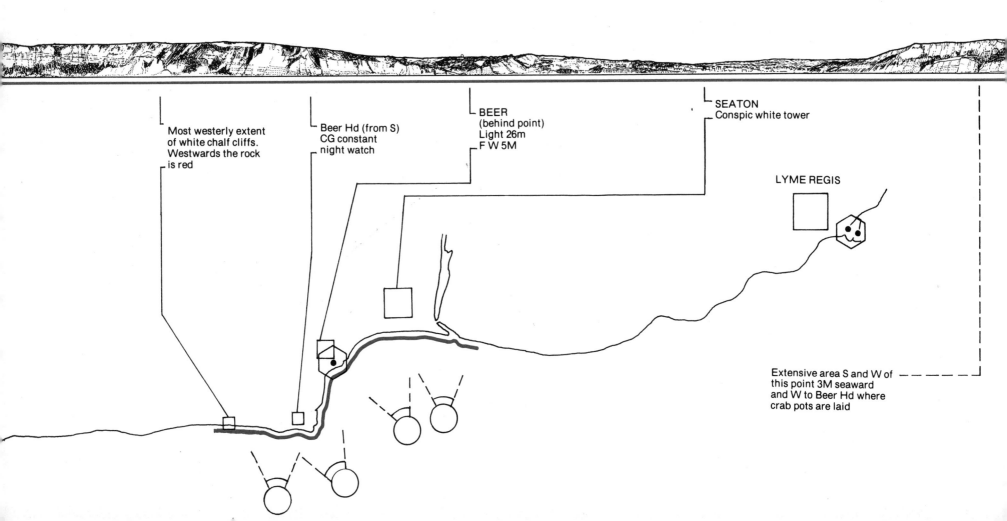

Most westerly extent
of white chalf cliffs.
Westwards the rock
is red

Beer Hd (from S)
CG constant
night watch

BEER
(behind point)
Light 26m
F W 5M

SEATON
Conspic white tower

LYME REGIS

Extensive area S and W of
this point 3M seaward
and W to Beer Hd where
crab pots are laid

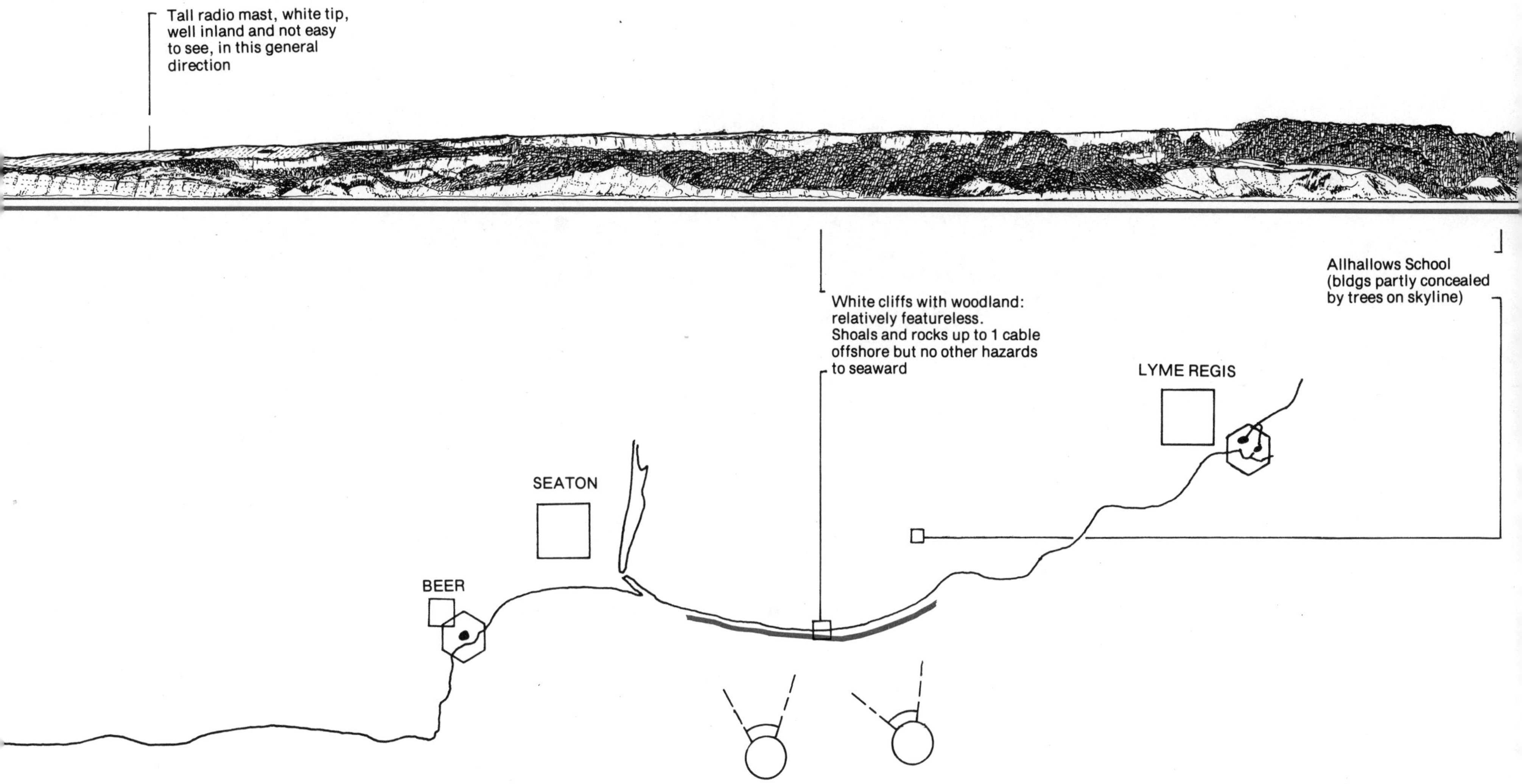

Tall radio mast, white tip,
well inland and not easy
to see, in this general
direction

Allhallows School
(bldgs partly concealed
by trees on skyline)

White cliffs with woodland:
relatively featureless.
Shoals and rocks up to 1 cable
offshore but no other hazards
to seaward

LYME REGIS

SEATON

BEER

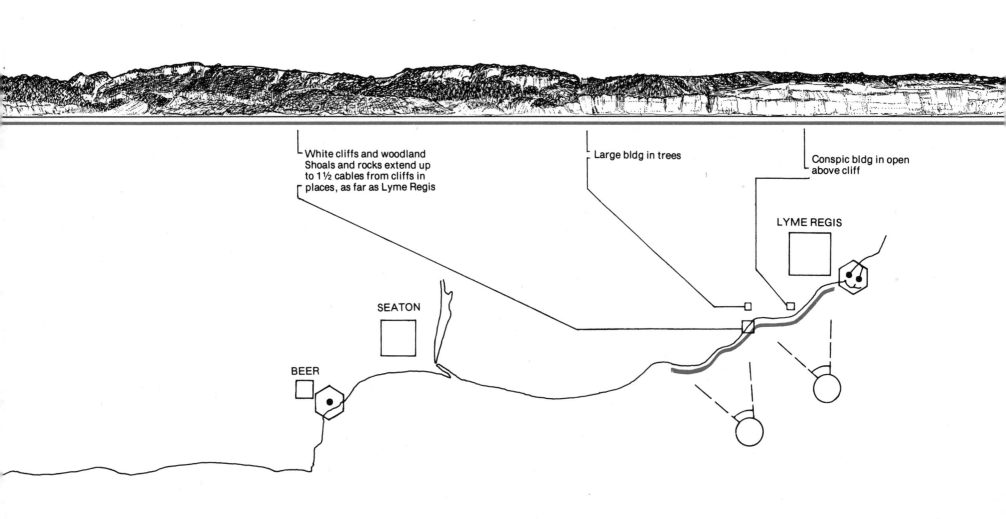

White cliffs and woodland
Shoals and rocks extend up
to 1½ cables from cliffs in
places, as far as Lyme Regis

Large bldg in trees

Conspic bldg in open
above cliff

LYME REGIS

SEATON

BEER

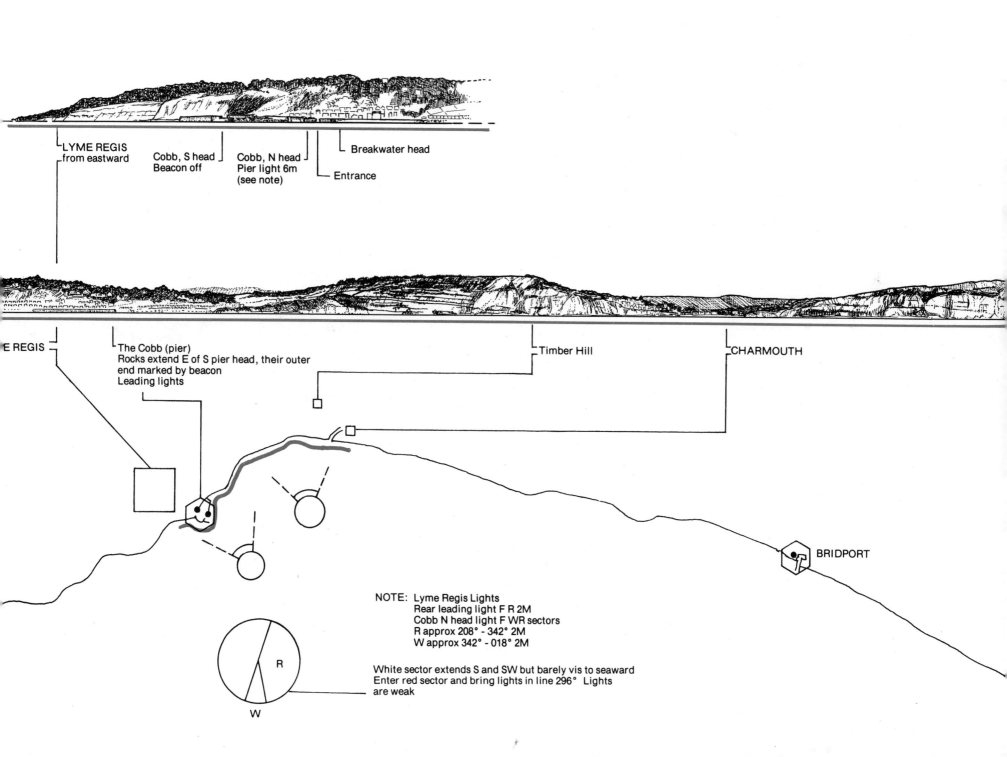

LYME REGIS
from eastward

Cobb, S head
Beacon off

Cobb, N head
Pier light 6m
(see note)

Breakwater head

Entrance

E REGIS

The Cobb (pier)
Rocks extend E of S pier head, their outer
end marked by beacon
Leading lights

Timber Hill

CHARMOUTH

BRIDPORT

NOTE: Lyme Regis Lights
Rear leading light F R 2M
Cobb N head light F WR sectors
R approx 208° - 342° 2M
W approx 342° - 018° 2M

White sector extends S and SW but barely vis to seaward
Enter red sector and bring lights in line 296° Lights
are weak

R

W

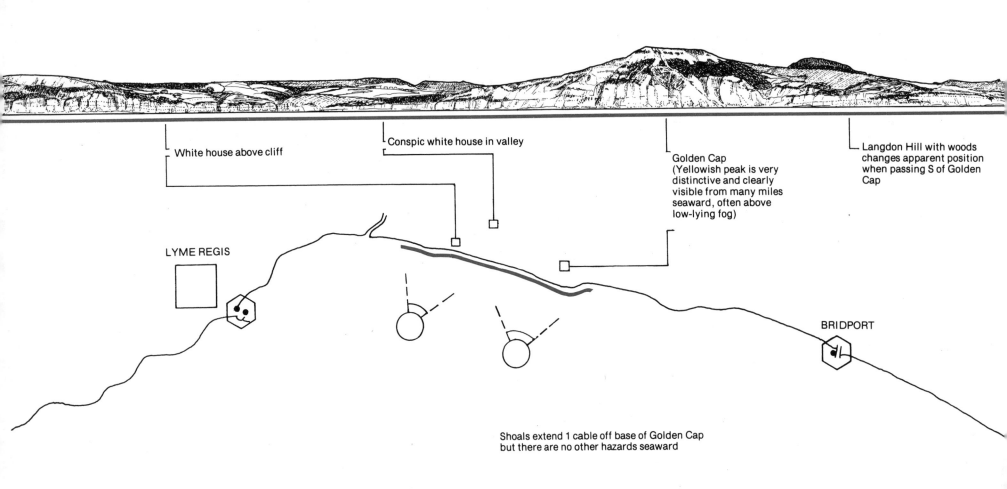

White house above cliff

Conspic white house in valley

Golden Cap
(Yellowish peak is very
distinctive and clearly
visible from many miles
seaward, often above
low-lying fog)

Langdon Hill with woods
changes apparent position
when passing S of Golden
Cap

LYME REGIS

BRIDPORT

Shoals extend 1 cable off base of Golden Cap
but there are no other hazards seaward

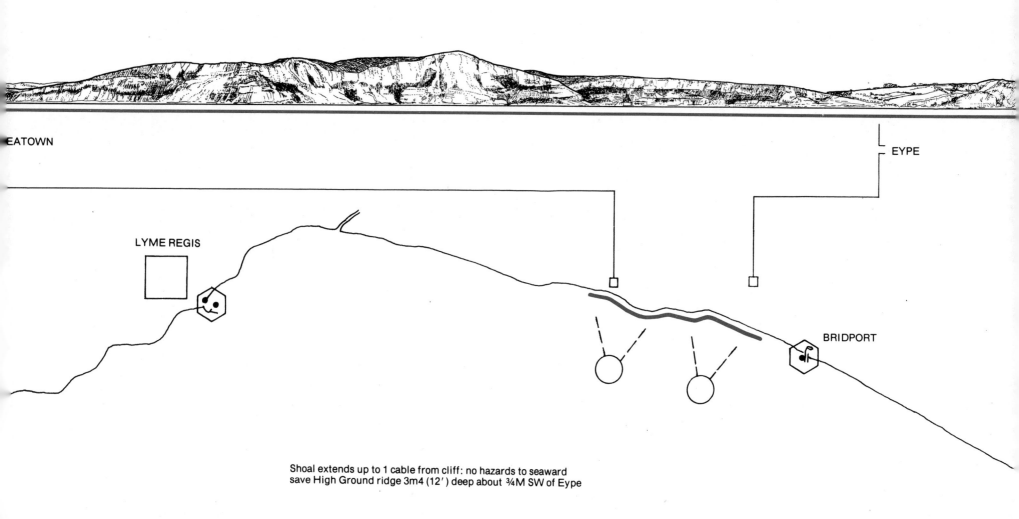

EATOWN

EYPE

LYME REGIS

BRIDPORT

Shoal extends up to 1 cable from cliff: no hazards to seaward
save High Ground ridge 3m4 (12′) deep about ¾M SW of Eype

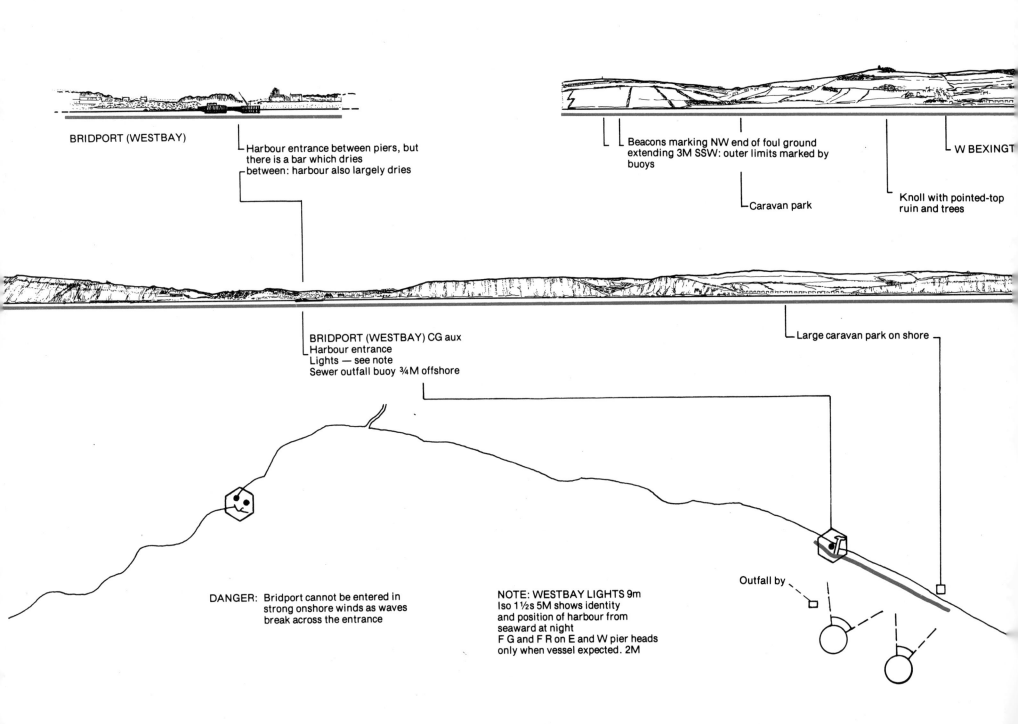

BRIDPORT (WESTBAY)

└ Harbour entrance between piers, but
there is a bar which dries
┌ between: harbour also largely dries

└ Beacons marking NW end of foul ground
extending 3M SSW: outer limits marked by
buoys

└ W BEXINGT

└ Caravan park

└ Knoll with pointed-top
ruin and trees

BRIDPORT (WESTBAY) CG aux
Harbour entrance
Lights — see note
Sewer outfall buoy ¾ M offshore

└ Large caravan park on shore

DANGER: Bridport cannot be entered in
strong onshore winds as waves
break across the entrance

NOTE: WESTBAY LIGHTS 9m
Iso 1½s 5M shows identity
and position of harbour from
seaward at night
F G and F R on E and W pier heads
only when vessel expected. 2M

Outfall by

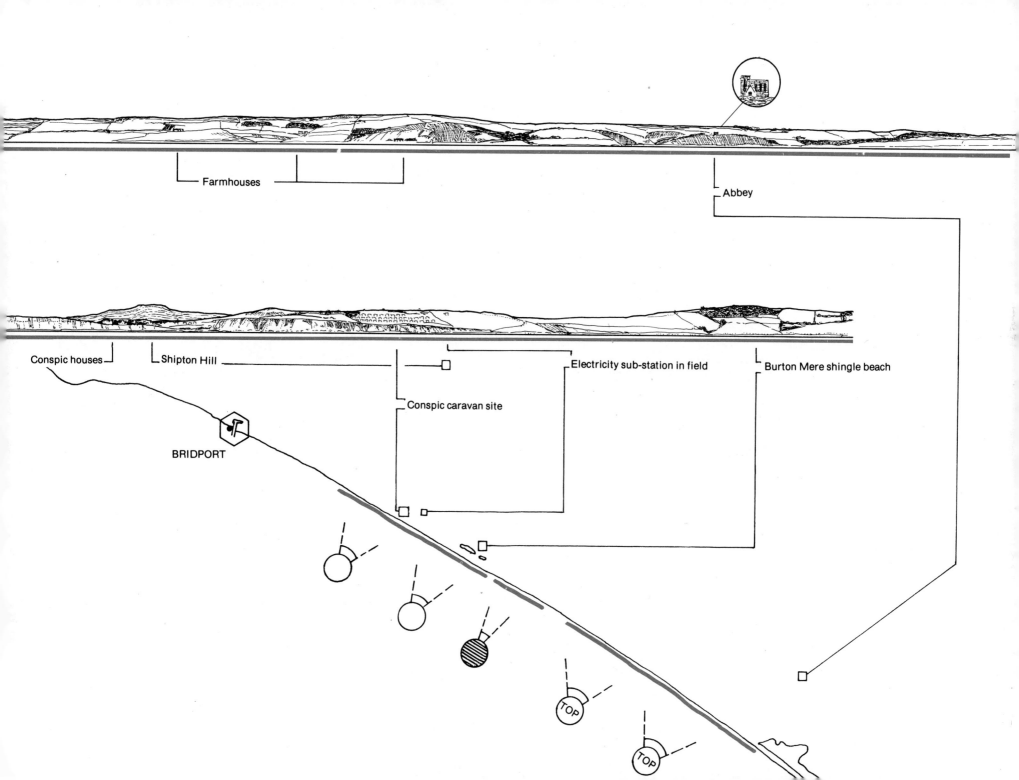

Farmhouses

Abbey

Conspic houses

Shipton Hill

Conspic caravan site

Electricity sub-station in field

Burton Mere shingle beach

BRIDPORT

TOP

TOP

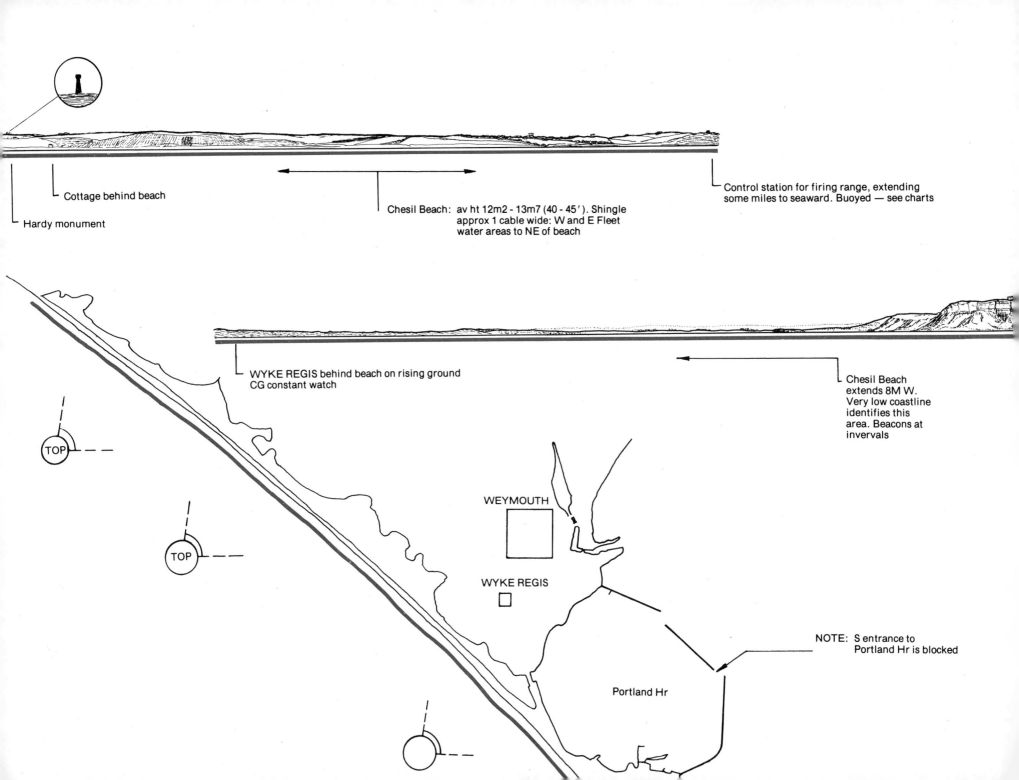

Cottage behind beach

Hardy monument

Chesil Beach: av ht 12m2 - 13m7 (40 - 45'). Shingle approx 1 cable wide: W and E Fleet water areas to NE of beach

Control station for firing range, extending some miles to seaward. Buoyed — see charts

WYKE REGIS behind beach on rising ground CG constant watch

Chesil Beach extends 8M W. Very low coastline identifies this area. Beacons at invervals

TOP

TOP

WEYMOUTH

WYKE REGIS

Portland Hr

NOTE: S entrance to Portland Hr is blocked

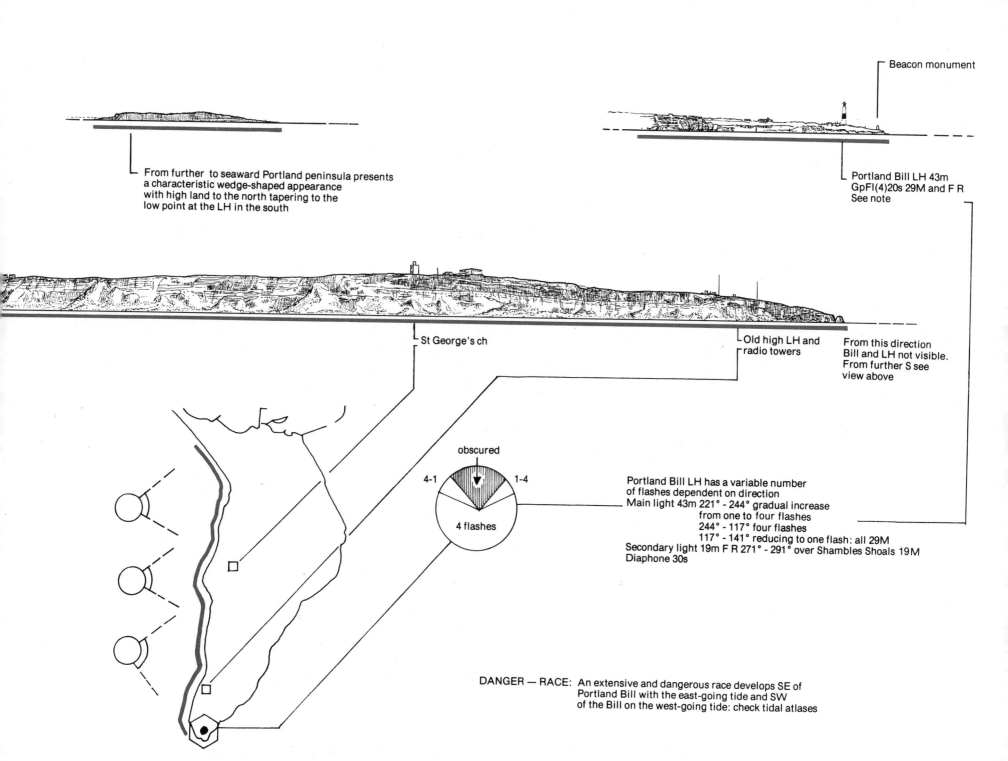

Beacon monument

From further to seaward Portland peninsula presents a characteristic wedge-shaped appearance with high land to the north tapering to the low point at the LH in the south

Portland Bill LH 43m GpFl(4)20s 29M and F R See note

St George's ch

Old high LH and radio towers

From this direction Bill and LH not visible. From further S see view above

obscured

4-1   1-4

4 flashes

Portland Bill LH has a variable number of flashes dependent on direction
Main light 43m 221° - 244° gradual increase
from one to four flashes
244° - 117° four flashes
117° - 141° reducing to one flash: all 29M
Secondary light 19m F R 271° - 291° over Shambles Shoals 19M
Diaphone 30s

DANGER — RACE: An extensive and dangerous race develops SE of Portland Bill with the east-going tide and SW of the Bill on the west-going tide: check tidal atlases

Portland Bill from westward

Portland Bill from southward

Portland Bill from eastward

To PORTLAND and WEYMOUTH

ROUNDING THE PORTLAND PENINSULA: Owing to the Portland Race it is safest to pass the Bill 3 - 7M to seaward, clear of the race position as shown on charts.

An inside passage exists in nearly all conditions, less than ½M from the shore of the Bill. There is almost always a strong south-going stream both E and W of the peninsula which can carry an underpowered boat into the race area.

Generally speaking, the Bill is best rounded at low water.

Local advice from the coastguards should be obtained: constant watch is maintained on the Bill and the regional centre is at Wyke Regis